INSTANT NIRVANA

INSTANT NIRVANA

AMERICANIZATION
OF
MYSTICISM AND MEDITATION

BY

ASHOK KUMAR MALHOTRA

ONEONTA PHILOSOPHY STUDIES

HISTORICAL AND CULTURAL PERSPECTIVES

10 9 8 7 6 5 4 3 2 1

ISBN 1-883058-01-5

Library of Congress Cataloging-in-Publication Data

Title: **Instant Nirvana**
Author: Ashok Kumar Malhotra
Subject: Philosophy, Meditation, Mysticism, Cults,
            Emerging Religions and New Age Psychology

Cover Image: Kamakura Buddha
Kamakura, Japan: Photograph by Ashok K. Malhotra, 2004

Oneonta Philosophy Studies
Department of Philosophy
SUNY Oneonta 13820-4015
Phone: (607) 436-2456; Fax (607) 436-2653
Email: *philosc@oneonta.edu*
Website: *www.oneonta.edu/academics/philos.ops.html*

Global Scholarly Publications
220 Madison Avenue, Suite 11G
New York, NY 10016
Phone: (212) 679-6410; Fax: (212) 679-6424
website: *gsp-online.org*

The 2007 edition is dedicated
to

my beautiful granddaughters

Rayna and Anya

because spending a day with them is my

Instant Nirvana

and to
all those students from
SUNY College at Oneonta
who took

Yoga

with me
during the past thirty years.

The 1999 edition of the book is dedicated
to

SWAMI RAMA

who, during one of our encounters
in the holy city of Rishikesh,
assigned to me the title of
"Swami Rishikeshananda"

and to

DR. AJIT KUMAR SINHA

who introduced me to
the delight of philosophy and
the practical discipline of yoga.

ONEONTA PHILOSOPHY STUDIES
Historical and Cultural Perspectives

EDITOR IN CHIEF
Douglas W. Shrader

MANAGING EDITOR
Parviz Morewedge

EDITORS
Michael Green   Michael Koch
Achim Köddermann
Ashok Malhotra   Anthony Roda

Department of Philosophy
SUNY ONEONTA
Oneonta, NY 13820-4015

http://www.oneonta.edu/ucademics/philos.ops.html

CONTENTS

Contents

PART III

PART IV

FOREWORD

I first met Ashok Malhotra during the spring of 1979. He was Chair of the Philosophy Department at the State University of New York at Oneonta. I was a young Ph.D. looking for a tenure-track position. Shortly after my plane from Chicago landed in Binghamton, I was met by Ashok and his lovely wife Nina. By the time we had completed the brief fifty-minute drive to Oneonta I knew I had found a kindred spirit, an invaluable colleague, and a good friend.

The intervening years have brought more tragedy and triumph than either of us would have believed possible on that quiet May day. We both continue to teach at Oneonta, nestled in the picturesque foothills of the Catskill Mountains. We have shared dreams and disappointments, celebrated both personal and professional success, and mourned the loss of colleagues, friends, and family members. We have had long conversations over seemingly endless cups of coffee, sat in on each other's classes, presented papers at the same conferences, and co-authored an introductory text.

Thousands of students of various backgrounds, aptitudes, and abilities have come and gone, many of whom stay in touch with Ashok or myself. Whatever the context—whether on our campus or in his celebrated semester-in-India program—Ashok touches the minds, hearts, and lives of each student, treating that individual as though he or she were the most important person in the world. His wisdom, love of learning, patient mentoring, infectious enthusiasm, and simple zest for life touch nearly everyone with whom he comes into contact.

Foreword

As editor-in-chief of *Oneonta Philosophy Studies*, I was naturally delighted when Ashok approached me with the idea of preparing a short book about the Americanization of Asian concepts, practices, and experiences. As a native of India who has taught, lectured, and written about mysticism and meditation for over thirty years, his credentials are beyond question. Because he had been born and educated in India, but lived through the spiritual explosion of the sixties, seventies, and early eighties in the United States–having in fact been given the title of "Swami Rishikeshananda" by Swami Rama of the Himalayas–I knew he would bring an immeasurable wealth of personal experience and perspective to the study.

Equally important, of course, was what I knew of Ashok's combination of penetrating intellect and unwavering spiritual commitment. Steering a path between naive gullibility on the one side and excessive skepticism on the other, he deftly guides the reader through the turbulent waters of this period of our nation's history. Along the way he explains in a simple but clear fashion the background, assumptions, weaknesses, and possible reasons for the appeal of the most popular movements.

For a few years, during the late eighties and early nineties, the economic and social tides in America shifted somewhat. Many college students focused overtly on "getting a good job," material success, or the pleasures of the moment. Enrollments in the Arts and Humanities dropped. Knowledge for knowledge's sake, spiritual enlightenment, and even simple humanitarianism were luxuries the new generation seemed prepared to do without.

Douglas W. Shrader

Fortunately, from this professor's perspective, the crass cynicism, overriding materialism, and pervasive pessimism of the period were short lived. Much like their counterparts from the sixties and seventies, the students I see today are searching for a better life, in all the richness, mystery, splendor it has to offer. Many are still fascinated by Yoga or Zen, a few think Deepak Chopra has all the answers, but more and more are drawn to Tibetan Buddhism, *qi gong*, or any of more than a dozen forms of the marital arts.

Although the current text does not pretend to analyze or evaluate these more recent movements (Americanizations), understanding the past may help illuminate the present and point the way toward a more satisfying future. Personally, I find that four lessons stand out in clear relief.

> ➤ *First*, the spiritual hunger that Dr. Malhotra discusses in these pages is not a thing of the past. It cannot be simply chalked up to a rapidly accelerated birthrate, generational differences, or the idealism of this or that social movement.

> ➤ *Second*, Americans continue to regard "the East" as a source of philosophical and spiritual wisdom. As such, any movement with even the faintest trace of an Eastern influence is apt to gain both adherents and monetary support.

> ➤ *Third*, in repackaging Eastern philosophies for American consumption–especially when money is involved–there is a pervasive, perhaps inescapable, tendency toward oversimplification.

> ➤ And *fourth*, oversimplified and repackaged philosophies, no matter what their origin, provide at

Foreword

best a brief spiritual snack. Sating the hunger requires far more time, commitment, and study than any popular movement (*qua* popular movement) can reasonably demand from its followers. There is no shortcut to eternity.

Douglas W. Shrader
July 27, 1999

PREFACE

The phenomena of mysticism, meditation, and instant nirvana have caught a great deal of the public's attention in recent years. People interested in these themes are curious to know what these concepts are and how they are related. To meet this need, I have composed the present work.

The main body of the book consists of six articles, which were read at conferences. They were written at a time, when the Transcendental Meditation of Maharishi Mahesh Yogi, the Hare Krishna Movement of Bhaktivedanta, the Divine Light Mission of Guru Maharajji, the Siddha Yoga of Muktananda, and the Dynamic Meditation of Rajneesh, were very popular in the United States. Some of these articles are based upon my personal encounters with the disciples as well as my interviews with the leaders of these groups. All the papers have been revised to fit into the format of the present text. For a smoother reading of the book, I have paraphrased all the quoted material. Furthermore, I have enlarged the paper on "Mysticism in the Hindu Tradition" to incorporate the mystical ideas of both Tagore and Radhakrishnan.

The book is divided into four parts. The first three deal with different aspects of mysticism, meditation, and instant nirvana. The fourth part is anecdotal in nature and deals with my personal encounters with gurus and their disciples.

Part I, entitled *Mysticism in the Hindu Tradition*, presents a historical survey of various types of mysticisms in Hinduism. Discussion centers around the

Preface

sacrificial mysticism of the *Vedas*, the philosophical variety of the *Upanishadas*, the practical kind of the *Yogasutras*, the devotional mysticism of the *Bhagavad Gita*, the theistic type of Ramanuja, the religious mysticism of Ramakrishna, the evolutionary sort of Aurobindo, the aesthetic mysticism of Tagore, and the religious-philosophical type of Radhakrishnan. This chapter displays the variety and richness of mysticism in the Hindu tradition.

Part II, entitled *Instant Nirvana*, discusses the upsurge of Hindu groups in the West especially in the United States. Here discussion centers around the Transcendental Meditation of Maharishi Mahesh Yogi, the Hare Krishna Movement of Bhaktivedanta, the Divine Light Mission of Guru Maharajji, the Siddha Yoga of Baba Muktananda, and the Dynamic Meditation of Bhagwan Rajneesh. This chapter reveals the unusual missionary zeal by showing that some of these groups have stooped to using television advertising techniques by declaring that the simplicity of their doctrines and the ease of their methods are an instant cure to all the ills of the contemporary Western society.

Part III, entitled *Research on Meditation*, discusses Yoga, T.M., and Zen as the three most popular methods of meditation practiced in the West. The chapter examines the scientific findings directly related to changes in the human personality resulting from the practice of Yoga, T.M., and Zen methods. This section is revised to add the most recent research from 1990 to 2007. The next section presents reports of students who in 1977 participated in a six-week course on the theory and practice of Yoga, Zen, and Mantra meditations. This section is revised to add another set of reports from students who in 2007 participated in a similar course on the Philosophy and Practice of Yoga. Their reports indicate identical outcomes. A new third section is included to show the influence of the practice of Yoga and Meditation at a personal level. Section four that offers some evaluative comments is further modified.

Part IV, entitled *Encounters with Gurus and Practitioners*, deals with my personal interviews with Swami Rama of the Himalayas and Baba Muktananda of Siddha Yoga, as well as my brushes with disciples and practitioners of these movements. Since Sai Baba and the Dalai Lama have contributed a great deal to these movements, material on my encounters with both of them is added to this section. A summarized version of their teachings is also presented.

This book is neither a scholarly discussion nor an in-depth study of mysticism, instant nirvana, and meditation. It is written in a journalistic style to appeal to the general audience as well as the undergraduate students. Though Part I dealing with mysticism in the Hindu tradition offers a scholarly discussion, it is presented in a language, which will appeal to the uninitiated in philosophy. Part II, *Instant Nirvana*, is written with tongue in cheek, to show that the T.M., Hare Krishna, Divine Light Mission, and other similar movements, have watered down the basic ideas of Hinduism in order to appeal to the masses as well as have stooped low to TV style advertising techniques to sell their spiritual products. Part III, which offers a short review of the research on the claims made by the proponents of these movements, will be helpful to the non-sophisticated reader to become more discriminative of these claims.

Preface

Overall, the book uses simple language and accessible style to appeal to the undergraduate students as well as the general public.

Thanks are due to Gottlieb Jicha III for typing the articles in manuscript form and to Marjorie Holling for typing the manuscript to meet the publication deadline. Professor Parviz Morewedge deserves thanks for suggesting the framework for the present book, and for his editorial help and encouragement. I am grateful to Professor Douglas Shrader, Editor-in-Chief of the Oneonta Philosophy Studies, and Professor Anthony Roda of the SUCO Philosophy Department for going over the entire manuscript. My thanks also go to the editors of journals for their kind permission to use the previously published material, as well as to the editorial staff of the Oneonta Philosophy Studies for consenting to publish this work.

In the writing of this manuscript, I have made extensive use of all the articles, papers, and books listed in the Bibliography. Without their help in providing the content and direction, this manuscript might not have been completed. Finally, my heart-felt thanks go to Cynthia Hall who went over the entire manuscript with fine tooth and comb and to Diana Moseman for putting the manuscript in its PDF format.

Ashok Kumar Malhotra
July 25, 2007

PART I

Mysticism
in the
Hindu Tradition

Ashok Kumar Malhotra

The subject of mysticism invokes images of something mysterious, mystifying, or totally incomprehensible. To make sense of mysticism, we need to go directly to its core. To accomplish this, we must convert the question "What is mysticism?" into "What is the mystic seeking?" or "What is a mystical experience?" This change of focus will move the subject from the domain of being confusing and abstract to something clear and concrete.

A mystic is a very sensitive person who perceives the universe in all its kaleidoscopic aspects. Though no color, sound, taste, touch, or smell escapes his notice, this panoramic reality indicates an underlying unity to the mystic. This underlying unity is believed to be the divine spark embedded in each cell of a human being or in every atom of existence. The mystic grasps it as the "stamp of the creator" imprinted in the core of each being whether it is a seed, or a cell in the brain, or a thought in the mind, or an image in the consciousness. A mystic seeks to experience this "signature of divinity" in each aspect of creation and especially at the core of his own being.

Though the concept of divinity within is at the heart of mysticism, it is generally understood under the two headings of extrovertive and introvertive mysticism. In the extrovertive variety, the universe of matter, mind, and spirit blends together to reveal underlying unity and this oneness is experienced by the mystic as the presence of divinity in the external world. In the introvertive mysticism, however, the mystic takes a mental voyage within, by crossing the world of perceptions, images, ideas, feelings and concepts, finally experiences divinity at the core of one's being.

In Hinduism, there are many types of mysticisms: the *Vedic* sacrificial variety, the philosophical type of the *Upanishadas*, the devotional mysticism of the *Bhagavad Gita*, the pragmatic mysticism of *Yoga*, the theistic mysticism of Ramanuja, the religious mysticism of Ramakrishna, the evolutionary mysticism of Aurobindo, the aesthetic mysticism of Tagore, the religio-philosophical mysticism of Radhakrishnan and the "instant mysticism" popularized by recent Hindu groups in the West. However, all these mysticisms can be placed under the two broad categories described above.

Let us begin with a discussion of mysticism in the *Vedas*.

Sacrificial Mysticism of the *Vedas* (2000-1500 B.C.)

The earliest books, which contain both the philosophical and religious insights of the Hindus, are the four books of the *Vedas*. A delightful intermingling of Aryan and non-Aryan cultures culminated in the creation of the *Vedas*, which contain their poetic reflections upon nature. This veneration of nature changed in time, to a belief that nature was pulsating with innumerable deities who could be influenced by singing, dancing, and the performance of rituals. Any aspect of nature, which had a real or possible relationship to human beings, was deified. The deities ranged from Sun God to Earth Goddess, and from the Gods of time, life, and fire to the God of ecstatic drink, soma. The creation of a pantheon of Gods and Goddesses led to the development of a complex system of behaviors designed to propitiate the deities. Of particular importance were the rituals of fire and soma, which the Aryans had brought with them to India. Soma, the powerful stimulating drink prepared from special mushrooms, when ingested during the ritualistic performance of the *Vedic* hymns in front of the sacrificial fire, intoxicated the practitioners to such a point that they identified the spiritual with the intoxicated body.

It is possible that this expansion of consciousness through the use of soma awakened in the Aryans the spiritual instinct, which lay embedded at the core of their being. The worshipers, elevated by the intoxicating drug, became one with their chosen god or goddess. Distinctions between mind, matter, and spirit melted away as worshipers were united with the chosen elements of the universe. This transformation brought about by the soma juice might have given them the feeling of immortality as well as the vision of divinity within.

By this time, the *Vedic* speculation had conceived of the concept of Brahman: an impersonal power in the universe. This power, according to the sages, had manifested itself in the form of 330 million deities inhabiting every part of the universe.

The unique features of the sacrificial mysticism developed in the *Vedas* can be summarized: first, nature was regarded as pulsating with various powers (deities); second, these deities were the manifestations of a single impersonal force called Brahman; third, each person needed to acquire knowledge of the deities in order to gain access to them; and finally, the performance of rituals was the surest way toward establishing harmony between the performer and the chosen deity.

This *Vedic* mysticism paved the way for the development of the philosophical mysticism in the *Upanishadas*.

Philosophical Mysticism of the *Upanishadas* (1500-1000 B.C.)

The *Upanishadas*, the concluding portions of the *Vedas*, contain the philosophical reflections of the seers. During the time of the *Vedas*, sacrifices pervaded all aspects of life. Practitioners had assigned elevated status to rituals, by regarding them as having more power than the deities. If prayers were conducted properly, the deity invoked would fulfill the desires of the supplicant. The exaggerated emphasis upon ritual invoked skepticism in some and led others to seek the calmness of the forest to reflect upon the universal principle of Brahman. The peace to which these sages aspired was uncovered in this solitary contemplation. Here, they made their greatest discovery. During the meditative journey through consciousness, they moved beyond sensation, perceptions, feelings, emotions, ideas, concepts, symbols and values, into the core of their being, where they discovered the spark of divinity — the self. In the *Mundukya Upanishadas* this self is described as pure unitary consciousness where all multiplicity is dissolved and peace, contentment, and sorrowlessness are experienced.

The sages of the *Upanishadas* made the further discovery that this self was identical with the universal self (Brahman). As the sages directed their reflections inward, they experienced the collapsing of the walls of the ego, and the merging of their being into the boundless being of Brahman. Their meditation revealed the self to be an undifferentiated unity, both spaceless and timeless, and hence identical with the universal self. The experience of identity between the subjective self (Atman) and the universal self (Brahman) gave rise to an intense feeling of peace and serenity equal to the experience of sorrowlessness.

This state of joy was realized by the sages through concentrated meditation practiced uninterruptedly, and with complete dedication. Since this arduous path was far removed from the experience of an ordinary person, the sages believed that only a select few, those who had total faith and dedication to this teaching, who had patience, who were tranquil and intended to be teachers of this doctrine, would be allowed to learn it. Once a pupil was accepted into the tradition, a sage instructed him. There were two parts to this instruction. First, the pupil was taught particular rules of action and behavior and second, he focused his reflections continuously upon certain mysterious words, expressions, and formulas, which were believed to contain the truth of reality. The expressions chosen for meditation were: *Tat Twam Asi* meaning "You Are That;" *Aham Brahman Asmi*, meaning "I am Brahman;" and *Neti Neti,* meaning "Not This, Not This." Together, the three expressions contained the essence of the *Upanishadic* discovery.

Tat Twam Asi and *Aham Brahman Asmi* when meditated upon, would make possible the realization that Atman, the inner self, was nothing other than Brahman the external self. In the *Chandogya Upanishadas,* this divine self is identified with the essence of the universe.

However, the third phrase, *Neti Neti,* was offered as a warning to the initiate, that the experience of the unity of Atman and Brahman could never be expressed through the concepts and categories of ordinary consciousness. Though this unitive mystical consciousness was beyond description, it was believed to bring total joy, and complete fulfillment.

Some important features of this philosophical mysticism can be delineated now. Through disciplined meditation, the sages of the *Upanishadas* had discovered that the divine spark (Atman) resided at the core of one's being. The inner self was experienced to be identical with the external unitary principle of Brahman, and that this identity with Brahman could be accomplished through intense reflection on certain sacred expressions. Finally, this realization was the state of supernal bliss or sorrowlessness equivalent to salvation.

The esoteric *Upanishadic* path to enlightenment paved the way for the development of two significant traditions. Though both of these accepted the truth of the Upanishadic discovery that the divine spark resided at the core of one's being, they developed their own methods to realize it. In the system of *Yoga,* a step-by-step procedure was offered to experience this mystical unity, while in the *Bhagavad Gita,* a path of devotion was developed where an initiate needed nothing more than total self-surrender to god to accomplish self-realization. Both paths were constructive alternatives to the abstruse method of the *Upanishadas.* We will discuss the method of *Yoga* first.

Ashok Kumar Malhotra

Practical Mysticism
of the *Yogasutras* (500 B.C.)

By the time the *Yoga* system had developed, the *Upanishadic* view regarding the identity of Atman and Brahman was a well-accepted fact. While some sages had experimented with various foods, drinks, herbs, and physical exercises to achieve an understanding of the self, others undertook a mental journey to discover inner realities, which offered them the experience of immortality and limitless bliss. On the one hand, the experiments of the *Yogic* sages helped them create a coherent step-by-step procedure to achieve self-realization, while on the other hand, they developed a metaphysical system to provide justification for the mystical discoveries claimed by their method. Let us discuss the method of *Yoga*.

Patanjali's *Yoga* is the first most highly developed system of meditation. Though it discusses the relationship between meditation and human personality, its ultimate goal is total self-realization. Metaphysically viewed, *Yoga* believes in the two ultimate realities of Purusha and Prakriti. Purusha, designated by the phrase pure consciousness, is the essence of a human being. Prakriti refers to material existence and constitutes a person's psycho-physical self. A human being who is a combination of both the Purusha and the Prakriti, is prone to identify the former with the latter. This false identity results in human suffering. Yoga aims to eliminate this condition by helping the aspirant obtain discriminative knowledge of the two realities of Purusha and Prakriti. Once this discrimination is achieved, the individual discards the false view, and is united with one's real self, which leads to the attainment of the state of sorrowlessness or eternal bliss.

Patanjali's distinction between Purusha and Prakriti is comparable to the difference between self and personality. While the self (Purusha) is one, the personality (Prakritic self) is a composite of mind, five sense organs, five motor organs, and body. In contrast to the self, which is consciousness, personality is divided into unconscious material planes ranging from the gross body to the subtle mind.

Since the mind is the subtlest aspect of the material Prakriti, it is that part of personality, which lies in close proximity to the pure consciousness of Purusha. Because of this apparent affinity, Purusha uses the mind as a vehicle for its own expression. As the pure consciousness of Purusha descends from the mind to the body, the individual mistakes his real self for one or all of these aspects of personality. Since the mind is primarily responsible for this false identity, Patanjali focuses upon the purification of this vehicle.

The contents of the mind are called modifications or disturbances. They consist of first, the entire information obtained through the contact of the sense organs with the physical world, the classification of this information through concepts, and the retention and modification of this information through memory and imagination; second, our emotional reaction to this information; and last, the sense of possession through which this information is made one's own. Each person has a tendency to falsely identify the self with these mental contents. Since these modifications are responsible for constant mental disturbance and restlessness, one's mistaken identity with them results in suffering. To make the mind a perfect vehicle for the expression of Purusha, these modifications must be harnessed and eliminated. Patanjali suggests a step-by-step meditative procedure, which by fully terminating these modifications, makes possible the immediate grasp of our real self.

Method of *Yoga*

Patanjali's meditative method consisting of eight steps can be understood in two stages. The first five steps known as restraints, disciplines, posture, regulation of vital force, and sense withdrawal, constitute the preparatory stage, and are called the external steps. The last three steps of concentration, meditation, and absorption, which compose the second stage of the method, are termed meditative or internal steps. The first five are called external since they are directed toward inhibiting, controlling, and finally eliminating all disturbances arising from outer sources.

Our desires, emotions, passions, and sentiments are disturbances caused by objects or people. The first step consisting of five restraints (nonviolence, non-lying, non-stealing, chastity, greedlessness) and the second of five positive disciplines (purity, contentment, austerity, self-study, ego-surrender), aid in building certain mental and physical habits through which outer distractions are eliminated. Other mental modifications are caused by the physical body. Since one's body, is intimately connected to one's mind, any change in the bodily mechanism is bound to cause a corresponding modification in the mind. The aim of the third and the fourth steps is to regulate and control one's body and its functions so that no undesirable mental modification originates from them. After the disturbances caused by emotions and desires are restrained, and the body is brought under control through the proper posture and the regulation of the vital force, the mind is still receiving information through the five sense organs. The fifth step aims at the absolute elimination of these sense impressions. Since the mind is conditioned to direct itself outwardly through the senses, the sense withdrawal step reverses this trend by drawing the mind inward.

The external steps cleanse the mind of all distractions originating from outer sources and prepare it for the second and more difficult stage of the meditative method. Since the mind is completely oblivious to the influences of the outer world, it is in a unique position to reflect upon its own contents. Now, the contents, which the mind confronts, are of two kinds: first, the information retained and modified by memory and imagination, and second, the awareness that the information belongs to oneself. The three meditative steps aim at controlling and eliminating both these mental contents altogether. Once the aspirant empties the mind of all superficial modifications, whether caused by internal or external factors, he will be able to grasp the true reality of the self.

The internal steps are concentration, meditation, and absorption. They constitute the three stages of meditation in terms of the intensity of concentration. Concentration being the first step, is the lowest level. Here the aspirant deliberately fixes the mind on one idea, image, or a limited mental content. During this interval, he lets other ideas glide by, paying no attention to them. The more he is able to keep the mind on the chosen mental area, and the less he is disturbed by other contents, the better is the concentration. As the concentration improves with constant practice, the aspirant requires less and less effort to keep his mind within the limited mental sphere. Thus, he moves toward the second step of meditation. Here the mind can immediately focus on any mental image and confine it there as long as it wishes without interruptions from other mental contents. After perfecting the seven steps, the aspirant confronts the final obstacle. This modification is the ego sense, which is the mind's awareness of itself as a subject. In the absorption stage, this interruption is eliminated completely. Thus, absorption marks the suspension of all ordinary mental activity and the aspirant experiences the real self (Purusha) as pure consciousness.

In *Yoga* terminology, this enlightenment is called *kaivalya*. When the realization occurs, the aspirant grasps the two independent realities of Purusha as the essential self and Prakriti as the non-self. This discriminative knowledge is subjective, i.e. the aspirant knows now that he is not the body or the Prakritic self and the Prakritic self is not he. Furthermore, he realizes that he is Purusha who uses the body and mental faculties as instruments but is not identical with them. This realization leads the aspirant to transcend sorrows, anxieties, and miseries of ordinary life, and to attain total rapture and complete freedom.

Though an advance was made when *Yoga* systematized the method of self-realization, this technique was difficult and, therefore, could be practiced by few individuals. Other attempts were made to simplify the method on the one hand, and to harmonize the essential features of all the existing methods of self-realization on the other. In the *Bhagavad Gita*, such a syncretic attempt was successfully made.

Instant Nirvana

Devotional Mysticism
of the *Bhagavad Gita* (400-100 B.C.)

The *Bhagavad Gita* is one of the most popular books of the Hindus. Its dialogical style, simplicity of exposition, grassroots level of discussion of complex religious issues, and its emotional appeal, have made it a standard text on Hinduism. By harmonizing diverse currents of Hindu thought and methods of self-realization, it puts forth principles, which touch both the emotions and the mind.

The *Bhagavad Gita* concurs with the *Vedas*, the *Upanishadas*, and *Yoga* regarding self-realization as the ultimate goal of life. Instead of rejecting the ritualism of the *Vedas*, the reflective method of the *Upanishadas,* and the ascetic meditational practices of Yoga, the *Bhagavad Gita* assigns each an important place within its own system. It introduces the idea of a personal god (Krishna), who is all encompassing: the creator, the preserver, and the destroyer. The pantheon of gods and goddesses of the *Vedas* is regarded as the manifestation of one. Rather than worshiping various deities, reverential and disciplined devotion can now be directed toward the person of Krishna. Furthermore, the *Upanishadic* idea of Brahman as the supreme reality, which is transcendent and imminent in all things, is repeated in the *Gita.* Here Krishna becomes the god in whom all things dwell and who dwells in all things. Krishna is not only the infinite and eternal spirit, he is also a human being, lovable, and above all, approachable. The devotee need not reflect upon secret words or phrases to comprehend the mystery of Brahman. Instead, one needs to perform each action in the spirit of self-surrender and devotion to

Krishna. Though the *Gita* recommends the Yogic method, it finds the path unsuitable for most.

Generally, the *Gita* is tolerant toward other paths of salvation, but prefers the devotional method. Krishna offers his discourse on the nature of devotion (*bhakti*) in chapters 9 to 12 of the *Gita*. He describes it to Arjuna:

> Those whose minds are constantly and faithfully involved in showering love on me are perfect worshippers... Those who perform their actions for me, worship me with total devotion, regard me as their supreme end, and are totally engrossed in me are delivered by me from their birth-death cycle. By setting your heart on me, by becoming my devotee, adoring me, paying homage to me, and by making me your highest goal, you will ultimately be absorbed in me.

In the *Bhagavad Gita*, bhakti is seen as loyal and unqualified devotion to Lord Krishna. We can relate to Krishna by surrendering the fruit of our actions, by being a friend to all creatures, by being unwavering in sorrow and pleasure, by inculcating an equipoise state of mind, and, finally, by regarding Krishna as the beginning, middle, and end of all thoughts, deeds, and actions. Above all this devotion to Krishna must be selfless, dutiful, and without any desire for release. Because Arjuna is devoted to Krishna, regards him the supreme end, and is ready to act for him, Arjuna fulfills the requirements of a true devotee. Gratified by the Arjuna's devotion, Krishna gives him a privileged glimpse into his rarely displayed form. This supreme form cannot be seen with the aid of scriptures, austerities, or sacrifices, but only through devotion to Krishna.

Though Krishna's exposition of devotion becomes the starting point for the later texts of the cult, it is expanded throughout the history of the bhakti literature. Historically, the concept of bhakti is imbued with emotional fervor in the *Vishnu Purana* (6th century A.D.), and in the *Bhagavad Purana* (9th or 10th century A.D.). Here, bhakti is not just a humble and unqualified devotion to the Lord but the feeling of deep loving adoration, which the devotee has in the heart for God. This view was elaborated upon and defended by Ramanuja.

Theistic Mysticism of Ramanuja (1017-1137 A.D.)

In his writings, Ramanuja presented a philosophical justification of the theme of bhakti. He modified the Vedanta view of Brahman by infusing it with the prevailing ideas of theism and found no contradiction in interpreting the Brahman of the *Upanishadas* as a personal god. For him, Brahman was to be understood as constituted of god, the world, and the selves. He regarded the three to be interdependent. Ramanuja took the Upanishadic account of creation literally, holding that god was the creator, sustainer, and destroyer of the world. Through god's act of will, the world and the selves were created, and the latter depended on him for their sustenance. Moreover, god, the world, and the selves constituted a unique kind of unity. As the individual self controlled the body so did god control both the selves and the world as its body. Though the world and the selves were different from god, they had no other goal than to serve god.

While god was eternally free and blissful, all imperfections pertained to the material world and all suffering to the individual selves. Ramanuja argued that since the real nature of the self was similar to god's bliss, a human being's suffering was due to the ignorance of one's true nature. Ramanuja asserted that this state of bliss could be realized by following the path of devotion in one of two ways. The first path, which is of *bhakti*, consisted of constant meditation, prayer and devotion to god. Because this path involved both the training of will and intellect, it was reserved for the upper three castes. In contrast, the path of *prapatti*, which consisted of absolute self-surrender and complete trust in the mercy of god, was open to all.

The surrendering of oneself to the will of god and the feeling of absolute dependence on him was the surest way of achieving the direct intuition of oneself as a mode of god. In this intuitive realization, the individual self was liberated from both ignorance and egoism but was neither effaced nor lost in the being of god. For Ramanuja, individual salvation was not to be understood as the dissolution of selfhood but rather as an eternal blissful communication between self and god.

Ramanuja's philosophical defense of theism accelerated the development and the acceptance of devotionalism in various parts of India. The biggest boost both at an intellectual and grassroots levels came from the writings of Vidyapati, Chandidas, and Surdas (14th and 15th centuries) who popularized the love for a personal deity as the surest way to salvation. The bhakti movement came to full fruition in the forceful religious life of Chaitanya in the 16th century.

In Chaitanya's time, bhakti was understood as the only way to attain salvation. Some of the major points of Chaitanya's devotional mysticism were: a personal God was the guiding principle in self-realization. The intellectual and spiritual experience of ultimate reality was minimized and was brought to mere bodily, sensory, and perceptual levels. The focus of attention was the physical form of god-Krishna. The personal god was loved as father, mother, brother, friend, child, companion, and beloved. God was adored from all perspectives, and this adoration became the major preoccupation of the devotee. The statue of god was perceived as real, and the devotee, in one's waking moments constantly chanted god's name in order to dispel distracting thoughts, emotions, and feelings. God's image was not only appropriated through sense perception and chanting, but also assimilated through singing and dancing. When sensual awareness was filled with the image of god, it was believed that one would experience one's divinity in the being of Krishna thus realizing ecstasy or rapture. Sri Ramakrishna, a saint and child of Bengal, revived this emotional mysticism in the 19th century.

Religious Mysticism of Ramakrishna (1834-1886 A.D.)

Ramakrishna was a spiritual teacher of the Indian renaissance during the 19th century. He was a down-to-earth mystic, who practiced and preached a meek faith, self-surrender, and union with the divine.

His mysticism is characterized by a deep devotional love for the goddess Kali, whom he called the divine mother. He believed that the highest goal of life was ecstatic union with the chosen deity. From age seven until his death, Ramakrishna had undergone a series of mystical experiences. Because of the frequency and intensity of his ecstatic trances, he was called "god-intoxicated."

Ashok Kumar Malhotra

He popularized a personal kind of devotionalism. To be born as a human being, he upheld, was a rare privilege. The gift of life had only one aim, that of god-realization. Ramakrishna conveyed his teachings through sayings and parables, three of which are paraphrased below:

> Each person is sent to this earth to do an assigned task. Do everything by keeping god on your mind because he is the one who pulls the strings of life.

> In every action and deed, god ought to become the focus. One should fix one's mind on god; surrender one's ego to him; put one's heart and soul into action, and do everything for his sake without hankering after the rewards. Moreover, since god is watching each one of our actions, he guides us and will take us across the ocean of life and death. Therefore, take refuge in god; say his name during your waking moments; and make your love for him as strong as your love for material things.

> Believe firmly in the god's omniscience and omnipresence. He hears our prayers because nothing remains hidden from him. (William De Bary, *Sources of Indian Tradition*)

Ramakrishna warned that god-realization was not an easy task because it required intense love, perseverance, ego-less-ness, persistent devotion, and the practice of spiritual exercises.

Initially, he experienced his trances through intense devotion and faith toward the goddess, Kali. As the frequency of his mystical experiences increased, any significant or insignificant sight or sound could bring about the experience:

Instant Nirvana

One day, Ramakrishna had gone to visit the Zoological Garden in Calcutta. As he approached the lion's cage, he saw the lion in his majestic form, which induced in him a mystical experience. He saw in the lion's energy, the omnipotence of god. This ordinary moment became an extraordinary moment because Ramakrishna felt uplifted from the mundane into the world of reality.

He was so sensitive to sights and sounds that certain perceptual experiences could transport him into an altered state of consciousness. Once he was watching a parade, where he saw an English boy leaning against a tree, which presented to him the vision of the young Krishna. This transported him into a trance-like state. Another time, he saw a prostitute in a blue dress. This vision brought before him the form and purity of Sita. From then on, he experienced each woman as an incarnation of the goddess, Kali. (William De Bary, *Sources of Indian Tradition*)

When Ramakrishna was asked to describe his mystical experience, he asserted that the experience was intensely real and utterly complete. By this, he meant that everyday experiences appear to be less real and incomplete in contrast to the mystical experience. During the mystical realization, an individual's finite ego would be completely merged into the infinite. The person would feel like a cheesecake soaked in syrup.

He regarded the experience as indescribable and incommunicable. An individual undergoing mystical realization would find the vision to be so full that he would lapse into total silence.

The simplicity of Ramakrishna's mysticism attracted both intellectuals and others. Before his death in 1886, he had declared that India could play a unique role in the regeneration of the West by exporting spirituality. His advice was well heeded by Vivekananda who brought his master's spiritual message to America in 1893.

Almost twenty years later, Aurobindo echoed the same message by predicting that the universal religion of the future would come from India. This religion would be syncretic and all encompassing. Because Aurobindo spent forty years presenting this message both in his writings and through the establishment of a spiritual institute in India, we will discuss his view first.

Evolutionary Mysticism
of Aurobindo (1872 -1950 A.D.)

Aurobindo, the great mystic philosopher of the 20th century, offers a wonderful synthesis of Hindu spirituality and Western evolutionary theory. Aurobindo finds the present day human being ignorant of his divine potential. The goal of his philosophy is to help each human being to actualize this divinity here and now. This, according to Aurobindo, may be accomplished through the practice of *Integral Yoga*.

Aurobindo accepts the *Vedantic* position that Brahman, the ultimate reality, is pure existence, consciousness, and bliss. As pure existence, it is beyond all descriptions, while as consciousness, it is the power of manifestation of reality in various forms. Since it is of the nature of pure joy, the universe of mind, life, and matter is created through Brahman's blissful play. Through playfulness, Brahman descends and hides itself in various finite forms. The spiritual light of Brahman becomes more and more dim with its gradual descent, and by the time it descends to the level of inorganic matter, the spirit fades away completely. The entire process of descent is termed *involution*.

Once the spirit reaches the lowest rung of the involutionary ladder, it must ascend. This upward movement of Brahman, which is the spirit's ascent back to its real nature, is termed *evolution*. Aurobindo points out that this evolutionary movement of lower into higher makes sense only when one realizes that the higher is already present in the lower.

Since in a human being the spirit has evolved into mind, a person has both the potential and the possibility to become the supermind. This power to realize the divine mind in the physical body is within the reach of each individual. Aurobindo offers the method of *Integral Yoga* to attain this divine perfection of the human being.

Integral Yoga is a synthesis of all other forms of yoga. Its goal is the total development of the individual through the harmony of the physical, mental, and spiritual aspects of the personality. The practice of *Integral Yoga* aims at transforming mind into supermind and thus creating the possibility of the divine life on earth. Once a divine life is created, the personality of such a being will be governed by complete spirituality. Individuals who attain this divinity will help others to achieve a similar state. According to Aurobindo, this affords the possibility of a complete spiritual transformation of the universe.

Similar to Aurobindo, who offers *Integral Yoga* as a means to the realization of this higher consciousness, Tagore offers the realm of art and aesthetic experience to achieve this kind of transformation.

Ashok Kumar Malhotra

Aesthetic Mysticism of Tagore
(1861-1941 A.D.)

Tagore believes that the need for creating art is deeply imbedded in the human nature. A human being is a creature of physical, mental, and personal needs. Through physical and mental needs, an individual establishes bonds of necessity and knowledge with the universe. These two constitute the physical aspect of a human being, which is entangled in the world of necessity. But there is also the personal man who is independent of the needs of necessity. In this dimension, a human being transcends the expedient and the useful and forms a special relationship with the world. This personal man in each of us has personal needs through which a human being's love, emotions, and personality color the world and transform it into a kinsman. This "personal man" is the impetus for art creation.

Tagore pursues the motivation for art creation further by comparing humans with animals. The energies of animals are fully expended in self-preservation, whereas human beings are left with an excess of energy, which they use spontaneously for the expression of emotions and imagination. This domain of the superfluous in humans is the driving force for the production of art.

The creative activity described by Tagore through the "personal man" and the region of the surplus is further identified with the impulse of expression. This impulse, which is central to our being is called "personality." Personality consists of emotional forces through which we humanize the world and make it our own. Tagore believes that man's uniqueness lies in the fact that unlike animals, human beings are intensely aware of their inner self. Their subjective-emotional energy is not expended completely on the mere world of objects. This abundance seeks an outlet. Its expression is realized through the creation of works of art.

Tagore is fond of distinguishing between the needs for self-preservation and self-expression. The energies utilized in executing the need for self-preservation display very little of our real self, because here, self-revelation is not the primary aim. On the other hand, self-expression becomes the ultimate goal when we are overwhelmed by a deluge of feelings, which gush through our heart and long for expression. During those moments when we become oblivious to necessity and usefulness, our hearts overflow with the spirit's energy by coloring the universe with our human emotions thus forming with it a bond of kinship.

Here Tagore grasps the creative activity in terms of personality, which by its very nature aches for expression and fulfills itself through the production of works of art. The expressive nature of personality provides only the need for art's existence, but not its purpose. Tagore discusses the purpose through the immediate as well as the potential functions, which art serves for the artist and the contemplator.

Tagore observes three different yet interrelated functions of art. In our ordinary experience, we are not sufficiently sensitive to the richness and fullness of the surrounding world. The first function of art is to stimulate our minds to the degree that we become sensitive to the underlying reality of the world. Once this is accomplished, art can aid in revealing both the concealed self of the world and the "personality of man." Tagore believes that through heightened awareness, art can help the contemplator to reach pure aesthetic delight.

The second function relates to our emotions. Tagore asserts that we obtain knowledge of the world through perception and intellect, but because these two ways are impersonal, they are averse to the formation of any close relationship between a human being and the world. On the other hand, we can know the world more intimately and personally through emotions. The value of art lies in its capacity to convey this kind of knowledge.

Tagore discusses the third function in connection with his romantic view of the individual. He believes that a human being is a union of the finite and the infinite. The finite aspect is limited, whereas the infinite side, which consists of aspiration, enjoyment, and sacrifice, is inexhaustible. This infinite surge within humans seeks immortality. Art is instrumental in expressing this infinite aspect so that even in death, a person will not perish.

For Tagore the third function is the ultimate because it incorporates the other two and provides the reason for the creative activity. Tagore asserts that the personality of man, which is the divine consciousness within each person, is the source of inexhaustible fund of energy and is the reason for art. This personality is in the body but is not the body and it is in the mind and yet transcends it. Though confined in the body-mind structure, this personality overflows the structure. The personality has the paradox of being finite in fact but infinite in aspiration. It is mortal and yet seeks to be immortal through artistic expression. This personality is man's link with the divine because through it the divine expresses itself.

As the artist reveals this divine energy through works of art, the contemplator realizes the purpose of art by indulging in the appreciative activities called the aesthetic experience. Tagore believes that through the aesthetic experience, an individual can joyfully embrace the fullness of the entire reality.

Unlike Tagore, Radhakrishnan, who was trained in philosophy and religion, offers us a different approach to the mystical experience. He follows the route of the universal religion.

Religious-Philosophical Mysticism of Radhakrishnan (1888-1975 A.D.)

In *The Hindu View of Life*, Radhakrishnan offers not only an excellent defense of the Hindu tradition, but also discovers for himself those aspects of the religion, which have been of lasting value. In his Upton Lectures delivered at Oxford, Radhakrishnan argues that Hinduism is a unique religion because it is not governed by any rigid doctrinal principles. It is rather a way of life guided by the attitude of tolerance and hospitality toward all religions. These qualities are based upon an even more fundamental attitude, which is reflected in the search of Hindu sages as well as in their ultimate discovery. Hindu seers were not looking for a religion for their own people alone, but rather a way of salvation for the entire humankind. According to Radhakrishnan, Hindus discovered that religion was not based upon a book or an individual, but on certain eternal principles. An authentic religion is the religion of the spirit. It is not a creed but an insight into reality. Radhakrishnan builds his own view of the religion of the spirit from these discoveries.

Ashok Kumar Malhotra

Radhakrishnan finds three major characteristics of the universal religion. First, it is concerned with the discovery of the spirit; second, it aspires to obtain a direct vision of the divine; and, third, it prescribes conditions, which when fulfilled, provide illumination to the seeker. Radhakrishnan believes that the Hindu view of the ineffable nature of the spirit is correct. This view is present in other religions as well. The eternal spirit cannot be understood through the concepts and categories of the sense-intellect apparatus. Rather, it is to be realized through an integral insight. Radhakrishnan finds this direct experience of the divine at the core of each religion. In the various religions, it is clearly stated that the eternal being can be experienced through an immediate intuition. The idea of wisdom in the *Upanishadas*, of enlightenment in Buddhism, and of "the truth, which will make us free" in Christianity, are different ways of expressing the intuitive apprehension of reality. This spiritual apprehension unlike the instinctive or intellectual modes of knowledge, which is an integral insight, is available to each of us when we open ourselves to the call of the transcendent. In the *Upanishadas*, we are told that we should grow from the intellectual to the spiritual, from isolation to love, from unfreedom to freedom, and from ignorance to wisdom. This wisdom is available to anyone who is pure in both mind and heart and is deprived of any preconceptions.

The tradition of this direct experience of the supreme is universal. In all religions and in all ages, this kind of apprehension of the ultimate has been emphasized. The sages of all religions are unanimous in describing this experience of the ultimate in uniform terms. They describe through speech and actions this underlying unity-the sameness of the connecting spirit.

Instant Nirvana

Radhakrishnan calls this integral insight spiritual experience, which for him is distinct from a religious experience. The latter is marked by one's worship of a deity, one's awe of a deity, and one's dependence on a deity. In contrast, a spiritual experience involves the whole person. It is opening one's being to the call of the transcendent. It is a personal achievement characterized by the involvement of one's entire being; a state of ecstasy; an absorption into the supreme; and a fulfillment of one's nature. It is, therefore, the attainment of freedom, enlightenment, and divine son-ship.

Radhakrishnan emphatically states that this integral insight is available to each of us. All religions offer certain conditions, which when fulfilled create an environment for this illumination. Before enlightenment can take place, one must train and discipline the intellect, the emotions, and the will.

PART II

Instant Nirvana:
Hindu Mysticism
in the West
(1893-1985)

Ashok Kumar Malhotra

In the previous part, it was pointed out that before his death, Ramakrishna had charged Vivekananda with spreading Hindu spirituality in the West. Vivekananda fulfilled his mission by bringing a popular version of Hinduism to America in 1893, which was further modified into instant nirvana, by such popularizers as Maharishi Mahesh Yogi, Bhaktivedanta, Guru Maharajji, Muktananda, and Rajneesh. The movements lead by these religious leaders aimed at bringing the Hindu spirituality to the level of the general public.

Instant Nirvana:
Transcendental Meditation,
Hare Krishna, and Divine Light Mission

Unlike Christianity and Islam, Hinduism has never been a full-blown missionary religion. There has been no Hindu ascetic, saint, or prophet urging his people to spread the word of the Lord Brahman to the far corners of the earth. However, before the advent of Islam in India, one finds historical evidence indicating that Hinduism took its first half-hearted shot at becoming a missionary religion by extending its domain to the Indonesian Islands and the South East Asian region. The pseudo-missionary stance of Hinduism during this period had a significant influence on the people and cultures of those lands. With the coming of Islam to India, Hinduism's fledgling missionary spirit was temporarily interrupted. Hindu history from pre-Islamic days to the end of the last century fully shows a lack of missionary zeal. But Hinduism did make a second attempt to revive its missionary spirit in the last part of the nineteenth century. The incentive provided by

Ramakrishna and others, culminated in the thoughts and actions of Swami Vivekananda, who established the first Hindu mission abroad in 1894.

During his meteoric missionary career, Vivekananda espoused a popular version of Hinduism, which attracted an immediate following in the West, though only among a small but influential group of scholars. Because these scholars were some of the best minds in America, the West started taking India and its heritage more seriously. Once the missionary door to the West was opened, there began a slow and steady flow of spiritual masters from India. During the first half of the twentieth century the spiritual invasion from India left its settlers in the West in the form of Vedanta societies, various Yoga organizations, and spiritual groups. Though they did their share of adding their unique religious ideas to the spiritual stream of the West, they quietly blended into the foliage.

This "bullock-cart" spiritual invasion picked up rocket-like speed during the 1960's. Hindu spiritual invaders of the nineteen sixties started an unusual business partnership with the people of the West in the garb of spirituality. In his work on *The New Religions*, Jacob Needleman offered significant insight about this "spiritual explosion" in America. He asserted that these spiritual masters from India were unique in that they had brought with them their practical methods and unusual organizational skills unmatched in the West and the world. Their uniqueness and significance lay in their innovative style and approach, which offered a real challenge to the Western religion. Though the responsibility for introducing Hinduism's basic ideas to the West was due to the efforts of the Ramakrishna-Vivekananda Mission, and Yoga societies as well as the Western disciples of these organizations, the greatest contribution on a grass- roots level had been made by the Society for Transcendental Meditation led by Maharishi Mahesh Yogi, the Hare Krishna Movement of Swami Bhaktive-danta, and the Divine Light Mission of Guru Maharajji.

The speed with which these three movements had attracted followers made them unique and worthy of study. In America alone there were more than one million of these practitioners during the seventies. This "Western rush to the spiritual India" or "the Ganges flowing to the West," as some writers of the seventies called it, had caught the Jewish and Christian leadership in America unexpectedly. Ken Kelley commenting on the Guru Maharajji Phenomenon remarked in *Vogue* that no one was prepared for this onslaught of the child-guru who challenged the likes of Billy Graham or the Pope. Those who regarded this guru phenomenon to be a passing phase on the part of American youth were shocked to learn that this little kid from India introduced the fastest growing cult in the USA. Others commented that this mass scale religious conversion of approximately forty thousand a month was the most unique event since the scientific revolution in the West.

In this section, we will summarize the essential doctrines and practices of these movements and reveal their underlying unusual missionary zeal.

Maharishi Mahesh Yogi: Transcendental Meditation (T.M.)

Vivekananda believed that different nations had different missions. Since India was the land of philosophy, spirituality, and love, her mission was to spiritualize the world. He declared that India must start the spiritual invasion of the West during the twentieth century.

Vivekananda's advice was heeded wholeheartedly by Maharishi Mahesh Yogi. In 1959, he traveled to the "spiritual desert" of the West to advance the cause of the Spiritual Regeneration Movement, carrying with him a doctrine of "Creative Intelligence" and the technique of "Transcendental Meditation." The system advocated by the Maharishi was simple in content and easy to practice. It was a watered-down version of the thoughts contained in the *Vedas* and the *Bhagavad Gita*. The entire system could be summarized into three general statements: the ultimate reality was bliss-consciousness; this bliss-consciousness was the basic nature of a human being; and it was accessible to anyone who used the technique of transcendental meditation. The technique could be taught easily in its two distinctive aspects: first, one must realize that underlying the analytic mind was the source of calmness and, second, one could use a sacred mantra, which would take a person from this agitated mind to the creative calmness at the core of one's being. Since the natural state of a human being was joy, the Maharishi insisted that this state could be easily realized by anyone who learned transcendental meditation from an authorized teacher. The necessity of personal guidance was emphasized because only a teacher trained by the Spiritual Regeneration Movement was qualified to provide the aspirant with a mantra in harmony with the latter's personality, to teach the use of the mantra to experience the subtle states of thinking and, finally, to check one's experiences as one continued the practice.

The attractive features of transcendental meditation were its simplicity and mechanization. The Maharishi told a reporter that he had mechanized the whole thing. As there were many kinds of blood specimens, so were the sounds for persons. These different sounds or mantras matched with different personalities. Once the match was established, the person using the mantra would be able to go into the depth of his being and experience instant calmness. The simple structure of the Maharishi's teaching captured the tension-ridden Westerners because it offered them a method to achieve instant nirvana without having to renounce their way of life. Followers were drawn to it because it was accessible, required no preparation, asked no rejection of the past, and no resolutions for the future. This here and now, self-centered, bliss philosophy was congruent with the hedonism of the West. It offered an appeal to the people of a technological society because it promised them worldly joy, a restful sleep at night, and an extraordinary vigor during the waking hours. What attracted a deluge of followers was the exaggerated claim that transcendental meditation could provide a realm of experience, which till now was accessible only to the sages or saints.

Bhaktivedanta Prabhupada: Hare Krishna Movement

Maharishi Mahesh Yogi was not the only Hindu missionary who offered instant nirvana to the alienated, insecure, and spiritually hollow generation of the sixties. In 1965, there arrived in New York another devotee and messenger of Lord Krishna who promised bliss through the adoption of the completely alien style of a devotee of Krishna. Swami Bhaktivedanta, the founder of the International Society for Krishna Consciousness, also called Hare Krishna Movement, did not bring with him from India another watered-down doctrine but the hard line Chaitanya Krishnaite sect of Hinduism. Since this sect was part of the Hindu Devotional Movement, its doctrine and method can be stated simply: Krishna is the supreme personal god and the ultimate object of our desire; the purpose of human life is to transcend the trappings of this material world of illusion and suffering, in order to live constantly in ecstasy through a devotional companionship with Krishna; and this supernal bliss can be realized by dancing and chanting the mahamantra as well as through participation in the ritualistic practices of the Society.

Unlike the liberal stance of the Transcendental Meditation Movement, the International Society for Krishna Consciousness was extremely conservative in its interpretation of Hinduism. Swami Bhaktivedanta assured the devotee of bliss only through structured work and strict discipline. Initiation into the sect was performed under the guidance of the Spiritual Master. Once accepted, the devotee had to follow four strict rules: no gambling or gossiping, no intoxicants, no eating of meat, egg or fish, and no illicit sex. Sex was permitted for procreation and having children to be raised in the Krishna consciousness. The positive rules of conduct were: the chanting of the mahamantra, reading and talking about Krishna, telling the beads, accepting a bonafide spiritual master, fasting on certain days, pledging to sacrifice everything material for Krishna, and finally shunning the company of non-Krishna devotees. With the exception of homosexuals and drug users, membership was open to anyone who was willing to follow the minimum rules of discipline set by the Society.

Because of its strict discipline and religious orthodoxy, the movement attracted a moderate following. But full-fledged devotees received maximum benefit because, according to J. Stillson Judah, this movement had offered the insecure alienated youths of the Western society, a stable religious family, which was dependent upon the strict routine, discipline, and religious zest. This structured life helped them overcome the sense of insecurity caused by the changing cultural values and roles. The Hare Krishna Movement was instrumental in imparting a purpose to the alienated, taking some people off drugs, reducing the crime rate among youth, providing them with faith, and an alternative style of life.

Guru Maharajji: Divine Light Mission

While the devotees were busy spreading Krishna Consciousness in some of the major cities and university campuses in the United States, there arrived from India the Bal-Bhagvan (Child-God), who described himself as the embodiment of the primordial vibrations of the universe. His followers declared him to be the Perfect Master, the embodiment of all past messiahs. The boy messiah was hailed "Lord of the Universe," "King of Peace," "Divine Incarnation," and "Supreme Boss." The guru founded the Divine Light Mission whose goal was to provide followers with an immediate experience of light, bliss, and peace. The motto of Bal-Bhagvan was: "Shower love on me and I will provide you instant bliss." He promised to make this instant nirvana possible through sacred knowledge to be imparted in four steps. Before this knowledge could be imparted, the guru performed a secret rite, which was not to be revealed to anyone else. If one did, this person would be demoted in his next life to a lower stage of existence. After that promise was taken, the guru taught the initiate to see a dazzling white light, hear celestial music, feel ecstatic vibrations, and taste internal nectar. The aspirant could also be given knowledge by a Mahatma, a teacher trained by the Guru. The teacher carried the initiate through the knowledge ceremony, helping him/her to see cosmic light by the ritualistic pressing of the forehead with thumb and fingers while the eyes remained closed; to hear divine harmonies by pressing thumbs in ears and index fingers in eyes and by gradually releasing the pressure on the right ear; to taste divine elixir through touching the top of the throat with one's tongue; and to feel ecstatic vibrations through breathing exercises and meditation. This existential experience was called "blissing out" or "instant nirvana."

The mission of Guru Maharajji was extremely successful because by picking up the dropouts of the sixties movements, he was able to pass them through the spiritual assembly line, which offered instant enlightenment. He attracted a conglomerate of followers: people disenchanted from the counter-culture and protest movements of the nineteen sixties, organic food lovers, flower children, and alienated youths. His followers believed that the guru had provided the skeptical non-believing western believers with an instant blissful experience of the divine through the eyes, ears, tongue, and body.

Vivekananda had repeatedly said that each race had a special mission on this earth. Some were born for the military power while others for the political greatness, whereas the mission given to India was that of the spiritual light. India must light up the path of the world with spirituality.

Vivekananda had summed up his message of the spiritual light in a few statements such as: belief in one's divinity, infinite purity, bliss, freedom, and love; belief in the identity between one's self and the divine essence; and belief in self-realization through compassionate social service. According to Vivekananda, India was destined to spread this light spiritual to the nations of the West. Vivekananda who was a charismatic leader presented his version of Hinduism, as an all-encompassing faith, which incorporated within itself the central ideas of all the major religions. Though Vivekananda's assimilation of the crucial ideas of other religions enhanced Hinduism's appeal to the masses, it also watered-down the doctrines. Furthermore, through his inspirational sayings and speeches, Vivekananda presented himself as a missionary in action and spirit.

A quick glance at the doctrinal principles of the Society for Transcendental Meditation and the Divine Light Mission as well as most features of the Hare Krishna Movement concur with those of Vivekananda's interpretation of Hinduism. Since the content of Vivekananda's version is already thin, those of the Transcendental Meditation and the Divine Light Movements is even thinner. Are these three movements missionary in spirit? Before one can answer this question, one needs to respond to the more basic problem of the essential characteristics of a missionary religion. If one can delineate its salient features, one can proceed to prove or disprove the concurrence of the underlying common characteristic of these movements with those of a missionary religion. One way to approach this is to reveal those attributes of Islam or Christianity, which distinguish it from the non-missionary religions. The historical triumph of Islam exhibits the following features: (1) a charismatic prophet; (2) absolute acceptance of Koran; (3) belief in one God; (4) principles of equality and freedom; (5) the promise of a paradise to be realized on this earth; (6) the simplicity of doctrine, which is pure and consistent with reason; and (7) the over-bubbling zeal of its proselytes.

Clearly, these distinctive features are also manifested by the Transcendental Meditation, the Divine Light, and the Hare Krishna movements:

1. Each of these movements had a charismatic leader, one who regarded himself to be a sage, a prophet, or an avatar. The three leaders did not initiate their respective movements whimsically, but each declared that he was appointed by his guru to carry the light spiritual to the people of the West.

2. From their inception, each of these movements had accepted one or the other Hindu scripture. The overwhelming response they received in the West, however, motivated the Transcendental Meditation and the Divine Light movements to "de-Hinduise" themselves so as to reach a wider audience. Transcendental Meditation, which started as a variant of Hinduism, changed its sales pitch by declaring itself to be a scientific technique. The only link with Hinduism admitted by Transcendental Meditation was the Vedic origin of the T.M. technique, but its rediscovery in its present form was attributed to the Maharishi.

Similarly, in the beginning, the Divine Light Mission adopted the thoughts of the *Gita*, but later incorporated the Bible, as well as the works of the Zen masters. Thus, by including works from other religions, it had liberated itself from dependence on any one religious scripture. Though the Hare Krishna movement was based upon the *Gita* and the *Srimad Bhagavatam*, which it took literally, Swami Bhaktivedanta had imposed his own interpretation on these scriptures through their transcreation. Of these movements, only the Hare Krishna asked absolute acceptance from its devotees of the scriptures; only Guru Maharajji required that his followers regard him the avatar or messiah; and the Maharishi insisted that T.M. was the only method to realize bliss. Each of these asked its devotees to accept absolutely the scripture, the avatar, or the technique.

3 Each one of them appeared to believe in a unitary principle, whether it was a Bliss-Consciousness, God Krishna or the Child-God. For a religion to have missionary appeal, a belief in one god is almost a necessity, as demonstrated by the history of Islam.

4. Furthermore, these movements declared the principles of equality and freedom. They opened their doors to anyone irrespective of race, color, caste, and creed. Transcendental Meditation and the Divine Light Mission had something for everyone, be they teenagers, intellectuals, businessmen, middle class drop outs or natural food lovers. Once a follower adopted the method of

T.M. or accepted Guru Maharajji, he was more or less free to drop out if the desired results were not obtained.

5. Each movement promised a paradise to be realized on this earth during one's lifetime.

6. The doctrine and method to realize this paradise were presented in simplified terms so that they were easily accessible to the common folks. The Transcendental Meditation and the Divine Light movements had capitalized on these features by declaring that bliss was possible for everyone not only in one's lifetime but within a few years or even months. Guru Maharajji, of the Divine Light Mission, offered the direct experience of divinity to anyone without any abstract or logical discourse on god. On the other hand, the Maharishi, of the Transcendental Meditation, asserted that you were only forty minutes away from instant nirvana.

7. The followers of each movement demonstrated missionary zeal. The Maharishi, Guru Maharajji, and Swami Bhaktivedanta asked their disciples to spread their respective movements with true missionary fervor. The Beatles and other show biz people had helped broadcast the message of the Maharishi; similarly, the conversion of Rennie Davis to the Divine Light Mission was a boon to Guru Maharajji. Initially, Swami Bhaktivedanta had depended upon the exotic look, dress, dancing, and chanting of the Krishna devotees to carry his message to the streets of large cities and to university campuses. When the Macmillan Company offered to publish and

sell some of the Swami's works it helped the financial situation of the movement.

The above discussion indicates the missionary inclination of these movements. But there is a problem. The over-enthusiastic followers of these movements especially those of the Transcendental Meditation and the Divine Light Mission had stretched themselves too thin. In order to reach as many people as possible, they had stooped to television advertising techniques declaring their method to be the answer and cure of all ills. Slogans like "Try T.M., you'll like it," "How to succeed spiritually without really trying," "Instant bliss without renouncing one's way of life," and more, make one apprehensive of their genuineness.

Instant Nirvana:
Muktananda and Rajneesh Style

There is a spiritual explosion in America. The technological civilization of the West has created a spiritual "black hole" and the gurus of the East, like Alice in Wonderland, have become "curiouser and curiouser." A seemingly endless parade of these masters has been arriving in the words of one discipline, to establish an oasis in the spiritual desert of the West. For many of these self-styled gurus, America has proved fertile ground for their spiritual gambling. Indeed, by cashing in their spiritual chips, many have realized unprecedented material wealth.

Why are we attracting these spiritual immigrants from the East? Is our ready acceptance of their teachings a reflection of our social and cultural condition? What are the factors responsible for this massive movement toward Asian spirituality?

Instant Nirvana

Jacob Needleman has offered various reasons to explain the spread of Asian spirituality in America. The first exodus from the East came at a time when the Vietnam War and the Drug Culture of the sixties were at their peak. The gurus offered American youth a positive alternative when meaninglessness, alienation, directionlessness, and spiritual hollowness had reached their zenith.

The American social soil of the sixties was ripe for the spiritual implantation of the East. The disintegration of political authority, distrust of social and political leaders, the unjust Asian War, the irrelevance of education, and the general disenchantment with social institutions, created a ready field to be sown by the East.

Furthermore, some critics believed that the condition of organized Western religion made America a vulnerable target. The Judeo-Christian heritage both in tradition and practice, could neither meet the challenge nor withstand the pace of changing technology. Those critics thought that it lacked the tools to fulfill the needs of its practitioners. Hinduism, on the other hand, had an assimilative character. It saw no contradictions in the approaches of other religions and saw in them different perspectives to reach the same reality.

The atheistic philosophical climate of the twentieth century further led to this spiritual crisis. The existential philosophies of Sartre and Camus had revealed the human condition to be absurd and meaningless, but failed to provide a practical solution to this existential predicament. While the existentialists held Judaism and Christianity responsible for Western man's suffering, they did not offer answers to the human predicament in understandable terms. The East, however, appeared to have the winning formula: a clear and concise method, packaged and presented in salable form by a charismatic master. The time for the spiritual invasion from the East had arrived.

The first wave of Asian gurus attracted largely disenchanted elements of American society. Those who rejected the institutional authorities of parents, teachers, and political leaders, flocked to the spiritual centers of their new leaders. It was a response to what they saw as a "sick" society. However, the attractively packaged techniques of these gurus soon began to appeal to a wider audience. Maharishi Mahesh Yogi's T.M., in particular, was loudly and publicly acclaimed by numerous show business figures. What began as a fringe movement was slowly creeping into the mainstream of American culture. Terms like "mantra" were as much a part of the Midwesterners vocabulary as they were the Easterners. The first wave gurus: Maharishi Mahesh Yogi, Guru Maharajji, and Bhaktivedanta Prabhupada were now themselves institutionalized. Mahesh Yogi ran universities, while the other two gurus were engaged in business enterprises. These "imported" gurus were now as American as apple pie, but the "spiritual hole" they tried to fill still existed. It was left to the second wave of Asian gurus to fill this vacuum.

The first wave of gurus helped the disenchanted tolerate the climate of the sixties. Americans wanted not only to forget the sixties, but to turn a blind eye toward their collective past. It was time to adopt a positive view of themselves, to look to the present for satisfaction, in fact, to ignore both the past and the future in favor of the moment. Christopher Lasch pointed out in popular book on the *Culture of Narcissism*, that the prevailing norm among people had been to live for the present moment, by forgetting the past and not having any sense of history. This had become the distinguishing mark of the present century. People's main preoccupation had been with momentary joy and psychological stability. Personal growth through yoga, health foods, and jogging had become almost manic preoccupations for many Americans. This movement toward wellness rather than illness, feeling better rather than being sick, was a healthier way of looking at the human condition. People craved to live a complete and wholesome life, to put every facet of existence in its proper place whether it was job, material wealth, or sex.

Baba Muktananda's Touch:
A Gateway to the Self

Two Hindu gurus of the second wave, Bhagwan Rajneesh and Baba Muktananda, made their spiritual services available to the people of the West. Both started their spiritual ashrams in India. Of the two, the first to arrive in America was Muktananda, who on the invitation of his disciples made a spiritual tour of the United States in 1970. So successful was the tour that large numbers of followers poured into his Gurudev Siddha Peeth in Ganeshpuri, India. To meet an increasing spiritual demand, Muktananda's disciples opened a Siddha Meditation Center near Liberty, New York. Since the opening of the Center, Muktananda's following increased rapidly. Initially his devotees were largely middle and upper class successes who came to Muktananda for spiritual enhancement on weekends, indeed for his "blessings" so they might return to their careers with renewed zeal and creative energy. Although spending a day in Muktananda's center gave one the feeling of time spent in a rarefied atmosphere; there was nothing at all esoteric about his teachings. They required neither preparation nor rigorous training. What intrigued many disciples was that Muktananda came from a tradition of teachers known for their ability to provide direct experience of the inner reality.

Muktananda's philosophy was a simplified version of Hinduism. His central concern was with the inner nature of a person. Human nature was divine and this divinity was bliss. When one lead one's life without being aware of one's true nature, one was unhappy. The goal of Siddha Yoga was to help each person experience one's blissful nature in every action or deed.

Muktananda taught Siddha Yoga during "Intensive" weekend sessions, which were called the "Gateway to the Self." These intensives were supposed to quicken the process of inner realization. A two-day workshop especially designed by Muktananda activated the process of inner discovery. During this workshop, Muktananda helped awaken the energy in the initiate in order to experience the inner self. The weekend intensive, which consisted of lectures on spiritual philosophy and meditation practice had five parts: meditation, mantra, posture, breathing exercises and most important, *shaktipat*. Here Muktananda awakened the inner energy or the self in the disciples through his touch. The highlight of the intensive was of course the *shaktipat*, during which each disciple waited for Muktananda to perform this miracle of enlightenment.

Shaktipat could be imparted only by a guru who had become a *siddha*. A *siddha* was one who, through hard work and discipline, had developed the power of his mind to its optimum. This power was delivered to Muktananda by his teacher Swami Nityananda, who himself was a *siddha*. Because he was a fully awakened spiritual being, Muktananda could impart *shaktipat* to disciples through his look, word, or touch. In his book, *The Bond of Power*, Joseph Chilton Pearce gave a description of a young heart surgeon who received the *shaktipat* from Baba Muktananda. The young surgeon, who was exposed to repeated experiences of death in his profession, had become emotionally numb. He had practiced meditation for sometime. When he joined the weekend intensive, he was given the *shaktipat* where the Baba grabbed him by the bridge of his nose for a long period of time. This holding on to the nose made his thinking brain to stop and permitted the experiential part to take control. The surgeon felt the flow of blue energy from the Baba's hand into his own head and then into his entire body. Though his rational mind tried to fight it first, it gave up. Once the resistance was gone, his academic ego opened up, letting the constricted parts to be free and relaxed. The surgeon, whose mind and body felt empty, experienced an overflow of emotions from his heart. After crying for 15 minutes, he was cleansed of all suffering and experienced the overflow of love and joy.

This story is a classical account of *shaktipat*, a personal power so unknown to the West. Numerous disciples of Muktananda who participated in the "intensive" described their experiences in positive and forceful terms. When disciples were exposed to the Muktananda's enlightened touch, they felt real, strong, and transformed. This nearness to the guru while in the presence of other disciples made them feel that they belonged to a group of chosen people who were intense, exciting, and spiritually uplifting. The weekend intensive was an extraordinary moment in the lives of the participants (chiseled by the Baba's touch), which made meaningful the past and offered direction for the future. An ecstatic disciple told me that just as Buddha or Christ returned finally to share, to teach, and to help mankind, the possessor of the *shaktipat* returns to everyday reality of family, job, and friends, taking with him rich insights, vigor, and inexhaustible joy. Though to achieve this experience, Buddha and Christ underwent extraordinary spiritual trials, the disciples of Muktananda had merely to experience the Baba's look, word, or touch. In this predetermined spiritual setting, there was little for the disciple to "do," except to allow oneself to remain a passive creature, swallowing whole what one "saw" and "heard," while basking in the glow of the guru.

The transported gurus were aware that Americans often sought instant solutions to life's complex problems. They treated their American followers as children who needed to be spoon fed with "spirituality." Like the Gerber and Beechnut baby food companies, these babas offered spirituality in T.M., Muktananda, and Rajneesh jars where everything was diluted and premixed requiring swallowing without chewing.

Bhagwan Rajneesh's Touch: Dynamic Meditation

While Muktananda's disciples were still "blissing out" in the glow of the master's enlightenment, another guru, Bhagwan Rajneesh, was offering almost identical enlightenment through sex, love, and prayer to his Western disciples ten thousand miles away. Rajneesh, who had operated from India since 1970, suddenly decided to leave his

Instant Nirvana

Poona ashram in 1981, to set up residence in the United States. Rajneesh had sent his disciples on a spiritual reconnaissance mission to America where they advised the Rajneesh Foundation to establish two ashrams in New Jersey and Oregon at a cost of six million dollars.

From the beginning of his career, Rajneesh had been a controversial figure. His unorthodox method of enlightenment, his radical approach to religion and philosophy, his "sex guru" image, his claim to spiritual enlightenment without the aid of a guru, and finally his outspoken criticism of the Nobel Prize Committee, created conditions, which might have forced him to leave India in favor of America.

Though trained in philosophy, Rajneesh called his approach psychological rather than philosophical, and existential rather than theoretical. This eclectic guru had drawn from various philosophical systems, religions, and psychotherapeutic methods. He declared that the goal of philosophy, religion, and psychology should be the same. This goal was that of self-actualization and could be achieved through the method of "dynamic meditation." A human being for Rajneesh was a divided being: both a beast and a god. Though still an animal, a human being had the potential to be a supermind. A human being was constantly pulled by these two opposites. These diametrically opposed pulls were the basis of all mental confusion. A human being could not deny the animal since that was what one was, nor could one deny the divine since that was what one wished to be. Therefore, the present day human being was schizophrenic. Rajneesh's goal was to cure this sickness by bringing unity to this fragmented creature. He believed that this unity could be achieved through the technique of dynamic meditation.

All traditional methods of meditation were inadequate because they did not take into consideration this peculiar condition of a human being. Zen, T.M., and other methods could relax you, but they could not accomplish unity in the person.

Rajneesh emphasized that before beginning with the technique of "dynamic meditation," one must accept one's neurosis. One should believe that one was a repressed person who was molded by the society to serve a function. One should accept one's insanity. To be aware of one's insanity was a sure road to sanity. Once one was prepared, one should follow dynamic meditation in five steps in the order given below:

1. Breathing
2. Catharsis
3. Use of the sound "hoo"
4. Silence
5. Celebration

Step One: Breathing

Meditation should begin with ten minutes of chaotic, deep, and intense breathing from one's nose.

Step Two: Catharsis

After the practice of breathing, one should express whatever came to one's mind. If one felt like laughing, weeping, or dancing, one should display these emotions spontaneously. One should move with the flow of these emotions without offering any resistance.

Step Three: Use of the sound "hoo"

One should use the Sufi sound "hoo" instead of the Hindu mantra "om" because the sound "hoo" affected the sexual organs and aroused energy at the most primitive level of our existence. One should shout the sound "hoo, hoo, hoo" for ten minutes by raising one's hands above one's head and by jumping up and down during the sound production. The sound would move the energy upward from the sexual organs toward the higher centers. When this energy would arise, it would pass through the heart, intellect, and the spiritual centers of our being. As the energy moved through the heart, the intellect, and reached the spiritual center, a person would be elevated to the level of "the highest man possible." The goal of the human life was to realize this extraordinary state of existence.

Step Four: Silence

The first three steps were cathartic because they were oriented toward action. The final step, being the opposite of the first three, consisted of stopping all activity. Do nothing! Be still! Become a silent witness. Positive growth would happen. This was the stage of non-activity. In this actionless state, a person would experience union with the cosmic energy. Here consciousness would expand and become cosmic divine energy.

Step Five: Celebration

After one had tasted the limitlessness of divine energy, one should indulge oneself in a ten to fifteen minutes of celebration and thanksgiving to savor this deep bliss. The technique of Dynamic Meditation should be practiced individually or in a group. If group meditation were possible, the energy would be particularly potent. Meditation should be done on an empty stomach, with eyes closed or blindfolded, and with a minimum of clothing worn.

To be enlightened and to enjoy the benefits of an ecstatic existence, one must work seriously at following this step-by-step technique. But it was also available through the miraculous touch of the master. Bhagwan Rajneesh, who lived at the highest developed level of consciousness, could magically pass on this enlightenment to his chosen disciples through his look or touch. This miracle of miracles had been performed by Rajneesh on thousands of disciples in his Poona Ashram. Now that Rajneesh had come to the United States, he was making this spiritual gift available to those followers who could foot his bill.

One wonders whether this gravitation toward the gurus was merely a spiritual phenomenon. Some critics had viewed them as spiritual revolutionaries whose appeal was a natural response by the West to spiritual hollowness. Harvey Cox observed that those Westerners who had turned East for guidance had found solace in the Americanized Ashrams of the transported gurus because their own sterile upbringings devoid of warmth and close ties of friendship were obstacles to experiencing life directly.

Other critics dismissed the gurus as spiritual specialists, but rather viewed them as therapists in priest's clothing. Critics argued that the gurus capitalized on our national mania for psychological well being by intentionally couching their philosophies in psychotherapeutic-jargon. Indeed, one guru did not hide his penchant for the psychological. Rajneesh openly said that his approach to the human problems was neither philosophical nor religious and that his method to enlightenment stood on a purely psychotherapeutic base. While Muktananda called his weekend "Intensive" the "Gateway to the Self," some participants regarded it as nothing more than a weekend of relaxation. It was easy to convince oneself that a genuine effort had been made to add a dose of spirituality to an otherwise comfortable material existence. After the weekend retreat, one returned to the practical world complacent with the knowledge that one was spiritually and psychologically "together."

Finally, there were those critics who looked upon the "guru-groupies" as "self-indulgent ego-trippers." When the disciples at the "Intensive" or "Dynamic Meditation Sessions," were touched by the guru, their exaggerated sense of uniqueness, their feigned superiority, and above all, their supposed sharing of secrets of reality unknown to the rabble was nothing less than pure vanity. Narcissism pervaded all.

PART III

Research
on
Meditation:
Yoga, Zen and T.M.

Ashok Kumar Malhotra

The plethora of popular literature on Yoga, Zen, and Transcendental Meditation has made it difficult for readers to extract the relevance of these systems, their methods, and claims. It is understandable then that the casual and the serious students concerned with the effects of meditation on the human personality are often ineffectual in separating fact from fancy. Slogans like "Try T.M. you'll like it," and "You are only forty minutes away from bliss," have reduced the once exclusive discipline of meditation to a highly lucrative business enterprise. With books promising redness to pale cheeks, firmness to flabby bodies, restful sleep, and worldly joy, it is little wonder that meditation has achieved instant commercial success. The man on the street rushes to buy a mantra even when the price is more than $250. After all, he reasons, in a society where people suffer from queasy stomachs, high blood pressure, and emotional stress, $250 seems but a small gamble. And it is a gamble, which countless millions are willing to take.

Although the purveyors of the popular view on meditation have made vocal claims about its effect on personality, their approach is decidedly one-sided and incomplete. Since our aim is to achieve a comprehensive picture of the relationship between meditation and personality, we will discuss the scientific perspective. The presentation of this perspective will hopefully provide us with a more holistic view.

Throughout this chapter the word "meditation" will be used specifically to refer to the meditation techniques of Yoga, Zen, and Transcendental Meditation (T.M.). Though the methods used by these systems appear to differ, they all in fact, regard meditation to be a form of effortless contemplation. Whether the meditator concentrates on a number of breaths (as in Zen), or on a word, object or image (as in Yoga), or on a mantra (as in T.M.), one is involved in an effortless directedness of the mind on a given object. Therefore, our use of the term "meditation" is wide enough to incorporate all of the three techniques. We will use the term "personality" in a comprehensive sense to denote the integrated organization of all the psychological, intellectual, emotional, and physical characteristics of an individual especially as they are presented to other people. As a complex organization of the above elements, personality expresses itself physically, psychologically, and socially through changes in the body, brain, consciousness, and in human relationships.

The chapter is divided into four sections. Section I examines the scientific findings directly related to changes in personality resulting from the practice of Yoga, Zen, and T.M. techniques. Section II presents reports of eight students selected randomly: four of whom participated in 1977 in a six-week course on the theory and practice of Yoga, Zen, and Mantra Meditations, while the other four in a similar course during 2007. Section III offers personal reflections on changes effected by the practice of yoga and meditation. Section IV presents some evaluative comments concerning the recent state of research on meditation and personality.

Scientific Perspective

Until 1950, almost all the literature dealing with the effects of meditation on the human personality was theological, philosophical, or popular in nature. Scientists, assuming a "hands off" attitude, ignored this important realm of human experience. It was only recently that some of the teachers and students of meditation had offered themselves as subjects for scientific study. Swami Rama, Zen priests and nuns, Himalayan Yogis, and meditators trained in Transcendental Meditation, had allowed themselves to be tested under laboratory conditions to demonstrate the efficacy of their meditative techniques. Encouraged by positive findings, scientists who at first had approached these investigations cautiously began to regard meditation as a genuine subject for study. The scientific research indicated that meditation induced significant changes in the individual and social behavior of the practitioner.

Two innovative studies on Yoga by Threse Brosse (1935), M. A. Wenger, and B. K. Bagchi (1957) focused upon the physiological effects of yoga meditation. Their studies revealed that meditators were able to decrease heart beat and rate of respiration. Ananda, Chhina, and Singh carried this research further by measuring the amount of oxygen consumption and carbon dioxide elimination in meditators who were "confined in a metal box." They concluded that meditators were capable of reducing significantly their oxygen consumption and carbon dioxide elimination.

In 1961, Ananda, Chhina, and Singh collaborated once again to study claims made by meditators practicing the yoga technique that they could stay in a blissful state without being affected by either inner or outer stimuli. Their investigation focused upon the electro-encephalographic study of the brain activity of two groups of meditators. One group, during the practice of meditation was exposed to photic, auditory, thermal, and vibration stimuli. The second group had developed an unusually high "pain threshold" to cold water. The experimenters observed well-marked alpha activity in both groups. This activity during meditation apparently was unhindered by sensory stimuli. Furthermore, they noted that two meditators emitted alpha waves continuously while their hands were completely submerged in ice cold water for an hour. During this interval, however, the researchers did not notice any discomfort or pain on the part of the Yogis. Thus, research appeared to indicate that the yoga meditation facilitated significant changes both in the body and brain of the practitioner.

Japanese scientists Yoshiharu Akishige, Akira Kasamatsu, and Tomio Hirai conducted similar studies on Zen meditation between 1966 and 1970. A particularly enlightening study examined the responses of forty-eight Zen nuns and priests expert in the art of zazen (a form of Zen meditation meaning literally "sitting in meditation") and those of one hundred control subjects. During the experiment, the subjects sat in the zazen meditative position. Their faces were covered with masks and electrodes were attached to their chests or heads. During meditation, the priests and nuns were observed to undergo a number of physiological changes. Their rate of respiration dropped from the normal seventeen breaths a minute to five breaths, pulse fell from ten to fifteen beats a minute below average, and in some cases body temperature was reduced by a few degrees. When an electric bell was sounded during meditation, control subjects sitting in the zazen posture showed an interruption of normal brain wave patterns for fifteen seconds, but with the repetition of the stimulus, habituation occurred and the subjects ceased reacting to it.

Ashok Kumar Malhotra

In the priests and nuns, there was found to be a continuous low level response to physiological and emotional stimuli. All stimuli appeared to have the same value and importance, and were perceived equally regardless of their nature. The psychotherapeutic implications of this study were expressed by Dr. Kasamatsu, who held that emotionally disturbed individuals could derive maximum benefit from the practice of zazen. By helping the practitioner develop a sense of detachment, Zen could reduce the anxiety of former patients who were about to return to society.

With the introduction of Transcendental Meditation in the West by the Maharishi, the pace of research on meditation was accelerated. From 1970 to 1972, Drs. Robert Wallace and Herbert Benson conducted research to determine the degree of physiological and psychological change brought about by the practice of Transcendental Meditation. In the March 1970 issue of *Science*, Wallace reported the results of his study. The practice of Transcendental Meditation by subjects was found to decrease oxygen consumption and heart rate, to increase skin resistance, and to effect changes in electroencephalo-graphic measurements. On the basis of these changes, they inferred that T.M. produced a unique state of consciousness.

In an attempt to replicate the results of this research, Drs. Wallace and Benson studied the physiological effects of meditation on 36 subjects at the Thorndike Memorial Laboratory and the University of California at Irvine. In the February 1972 issue of *Science*, they corroborated the results of the earlier study.

Based upon these findings, Drs. Wallace and Benson concluded that Transcendental Meditation was not only conducive to significant physical changes but also made possible an altered state of consciousness. Wallace designated this state of consciousness as "hypermetabolic," which was quite different from the wakeful, dreaming, and sleeping states. The research by Benson and Wallace revealed not only the physiological effects of meditation, but also indicated the presence of a level of consciousness, which until recently was talked of by theologians and religionists, in highly esoteric terms.

Other researchers had concentrated upon the effects of meditation on specific aspects of the human personality. Lesh (1970) reported the positive influence of the Zen technique on the development of empathy in counselors. Meditation was found to be an effective means toward the achievement of self-actualization, i.e., an openness to experience and a self-dependence on feelings and values. In a later study by Curtin (1973), Transcendental Meditation was found to be related to significant changes in the subject's capacity to regress adaptively. The term "adaptive regression" referred to the ability of the individual to bring to awareness the inner self or more specifically, to the suspension of the ego's defense mechanisms in order to gain access to the unconscious content of the mind.

T.M. increased one's capacity for "adaptive regression" and could, according to the author, play an important role in the enhancement and development of psychological health. Studies by Seeman, Nidich, Banta (1972), and Polowniak (1973) reported the use of meditation in the self-actualization process. In the study, an instrument measuring self-actualization was administered to control and experimental subjects prior to and ten weeks after beginning a program of T.M. There were significant difference between control and experimental groups on ten out of twelve variables measured. As hypothesized, subjects exposed to T.M. moved in the direction of self-actualization. In the Polowniak study, yoga meditation was found to be related to significant changes in fourteen out of nineteen personality variables studied. Participants in meditation showed increased self-concept, greater purpose, and a higher sense of well being than the non-participating control group.

Linden (1972) employed T.M. training with 84 third grade students. His findings indicated that the training lead to greater attentional functioning, increased ability to cope effectively with anxiety situations, and greater achievement in reading. Studies by Boudreau (1972), Girodo (1974), and Shapiro (1976) further established that meditation could help to eliminate specific physical, emotional, and psychological ailments. In the Boudreau study, two cases, one of claustrophobia, the other of excessive perspiration, were treated with the behavioral technique known as "systematic desensitization" in which the client was asked to relax as he imagined a hierarchy of increasingly anxiety producing stimuli. In the above situations this technique proved to have limited success. Transcendental Meditation was then introduced in one case, while in the other, yoga meditation was used as an intervention strategy. Both techniques were therapeutically successful after systematic desensitization had only partially alleviated the presenting symptoms.

In Girodo's study, yoga meditation was used to decrease anxiety symptoms in patients diagnosed as anxiety neurotic. Following the practice of yoga meditation for five months, it was found that a majority of patients exhibited a significant decline in anxiety symptoms. An innovative study by Shapiro attempted to integrate the behaviorally oriented self-management techniques with humanistically oriented techniques of meditation. A case of generalized anxiety was treated with a combination of Zen meditation and behavioral self-control strategies. Training was done in a weekend Zen workshop; formal and informal meditation was taught, and the subject was instructed in behavioral self-observation. During the six weeks of the program, the subject reported a significant decrease in feelings of stress and anxiety. This study would appear to have implications for the integration of Western and Eastern techniques in psychotherapy. Furthermore, Drs. Wallace and Benson in a study of 1862 drug users, showed that a majority gave up using and pushing drugs after 21 months of practicing Transcendental Meditation. Their research suggested that T.M. might become a useful tool for fighting drug abuse.

Although the scientific research cited here indicates the positive effects of meditation on the human personality, there had been recent studies, which offered serious challenge to some of these claims. Because, most of the current research focused on Transcendental Meditation, a majority of critical studies were directed at this technique. Critics argued that since research on T.M. had been done exclusively by followers of the technique, studies retained a subjective character, which rendered them unreliable, one-sided, and even suspicious. Recently however, there had appeared half a dozen studies, which had countered some of T.M.'s prominent claims. We will briefly mention a few.

Two studies by Pagano *et al* and Michaels *et al* are the first to challenge the results presented in an article on "The Physiology of Meditation" by Wallace and Benson. Beside the physical changes occurring during meditation, Wallace and Benson reported the appearance of a unique transcendental state, which they called "wakeful hypermetabolic." Wallace argued that this state was unlike "ordinary relaxed or sleep states" and was conducive to stress reduction, heightened awareness, and an elevated sense of well-being. Pagano and his colleagues interested in investigating the appearance of this unique state of consciousness during meditation observed five experienced meditators under laboratory conditions. Pagano's observations appeared to lay some doubt on Wallace and Benson's claim of a "wakeful hypermetabolic" state. Pagano noted both through subjective reports of practitioners and EEG records, that the meditators spent 40% of meditation time in sleep. He questioned, therefore, whether sleep or some other aspect of the meditative process might be responsible for its beneficial effects.

The second study by Michaels *et al* challenges Wallace's claim from another viewpoint. Michaels and his co-workers denied not only the existence of this "hypermetabolic state" but also the claim that T.M. was unique in reducing stress. Michaels' study could be summarized as follows: blood chemical levels related to stress were measured in two groups. One group merely relaxed while the other meditated. Results indicated that the two groups did not differ significantly with regard to metabolic state. Therefore, biochemically, the state produced by meditation was observed to be similar to the state made possible by mere rest. Michaels concluded from his study that although T.M. could not biochemically reduce stress, it might produce beneficial psychological effects on its practitioners.

Instant Nirvana

Other scientists challenge the exclusivity of the T.M. technique while at the same time acknowledging its beneficial effects upon the body. Dr. John Laragh, a leading expert on hypertension in the U.S.A., questioned whether meditation's effect on blood pressure differs from the effects of other simpler forms of relaxation. Psychiatrist Stanley Dean who expressed the sentiments of a considerable portion of the scientific community acknowledged T.M.'s importance as an additional medical tool, but maintained that the method was neither an exclusive nor an innovative way of achieving mental equanimity. Studies by Travis *et al* (1976) and Pollack *et al* (1975) supported Laragh's and Dean's comments. Their studies reported that the physical changes, which took place during Transcendental Meditation occurred also among subjects who rested, relaxed, or used Benson's relaxation response technique. Therefore, most researchers had discarded the alleged distinctiveness of the T.M. approach.

Recent Research (1990-2007)

From 1960 to 1990, research on the effects of meditation on the human personality was moving at a bullock-cart speed. But more recently from 1990 to 2007, it had picked up rocket-like speed. Earlier, yoga and meditation were more of a fad and were not taken seriously either by the scientific community or the general public. However, the trend has changed during the past 17 years. Now there are millions of genuine practioners, who are willing to report on the results accrued from its constant practice.

Medical Research on alternative therapies such as acupuncture, tai chi, shiatsu, chiropractic, yoga and meditation, has provided this kind of boost. Though the research done at the Harvard Development Center on the alternative therapies has been catalytic in the enhancement of this interest and credibility, there are other factors responsible for the intensity of inquisitiveness in this very important area of human development. Five major reasons have contributed towards this serious curiosity.

First, following the lead of Harvard University, a number of researchers from other prestigious universities such as M.I.T, Cambridge, Toronto, University of Wisconsin at Madison, and University of Pennsylvania have got involved in studying the connection between meditation and its positive effects on the human body, emotions and brain. This has brought credible veracity to the scientific research in this neglected area.

Second, the much revered Dalai Lama recently addressed a gathering of neuroscientists, medical doctors, psychotherapists and psychologists by presenting them with a challenge of utilizing the brain imaging tools to map out the brain waves of the Buddhist monks, who had practiced meditation for years. The medical community accepted this challenge and proceeded with the research with utmost seriousness.

Third, the adoption of the techniques of yoga and meditation by the Hollywood actors such as Richard Gere, Goldie Hawn, Demi Moore and others along with such politicians as Al Gore, has further enhanced the current interest.

Fourth, Deepak Chopra, a scientist turned philosopher and a new age guru, who through his numerous best sellers on the topics of Hinduism, Yoga and Meditation, has played a crucial role in the enhancement of awareness among the general public.

And fifth, because of this popular appeal, a large number of people of all ages have flocked to the yoga and meditation centers thus creating a fertile ground for the researchers to get their best pick as subjects for the scientific experiments. All these factors have contributed to opening up of this significant field for the scientists, medical doctors and psychologists, who in turn, have conducted a large number of studies with positive results.

American society is super-saturated with stress. The obvious reasons being the news that we watch on the TV, hear on the radio and read in the newspapers or magazines. Most of the news has been devoted to war, innocent people being killed, terrorists striking the subways or air ports, murder and mugging in the streets of big and small cities, bridges being blown up, tunnels in grave danger, food and water being poisoned, crop being contaminated, consumption of beef and poultry could lead to fatal diseases and intimacy between two human beings might end up in AIDS. The news media is good at selling its product by depicting the horrible and sordid aspects of life and the general public is buying it and paying it with a great deal of anxiety and stress. To add fuel to the fire, the politicians in the USA have capitalized on the wave of negativity by exacerbating the situation by amplifying the terrorist threat. Furthermore, the 9/11 tragedy has impinged upon the psyche of the people through the primitive fear that Bin Laden, who with its brute irrational force, might cause havoc to the comfortable life-style of the civilized people of the West. All this has contributed to heightening the stress among the general public. When people are in this state of stress constantly, they look for a quick fix. To reduce this imminent tension, they look towards yoga and meditation as their panacea. Their flocking to the yoga and meditation centers is understandable.

The practice of yoga and meditation that used to be the playground for the rich and famous has simmered down to the level of ordinary people during the last 17 years. The results they found are of enormous importance for the stressed out members of the society. A plethora of research studies conducted by the researchers indicates that the regular practice of meditation results in the reshaping of the brain so that it could handle stress. Meditation on a regular basis helps slow down and eventually shuts down the influence of the conceptual part of the brain, which in turn offers the individual the freedom to pick and choose new responses to the existing situation. Moreover, meditation helps break the conditioning determinants of the society by relaxing their hold on the person. Regular practice of meditation assists the practitioner to concentrate on the present without worrying about the past. By minimizing the effects of the past conditioning of the society, the individual then is able to relax and enjoy the present moment with full intensity.

Studies have also shown that when people meditate for ten to fifteen minutes on a mantra or concentrate on breathing or the diaphragm or silence, they experience relaxation and a sense of well being unparallel to any state of relaxation they felt before.

The popularity of yoga and meditation caught the eyes of Time Magazine, which in its August 4, 2003 issue devoted the section on *Health* to the effects of meditation on the human personality. The article reiterates *stress* as one of the major health problems in the American society. Lives of officials driven by stiff competition are inundated with enormous nervous tension and anxiety. Research studies have shown that a few minutes of regular practice of meditation enhances the immune system by rewiring the brain resulting in stress and anxiety reduction. Officials whose lives are hectic are able to take control of their well being through a daily dosage of meditation.

The Dalai Lama's challenge to the Western scientist was well heeded and the research on mapping the brain imaging of the expert meditators has been seriously documented. By the efficient use of the brain imaging technology, scientists and researchers were able to produce positive findings. Their results indicated that the states of the brain resulting from the meditative experience were not mystifying but could be displayed in rainbow colors. Moreover their results indicated that significant changes occurred among both the expert meditators as well as the beginners.

Studies showed that even the beginners in meditation revealed less activity in their frontal cortex, which is the seat of such complex functions as reasoning, planning, emotions, personal identity and self-consciousness. The first time meditators found that this part of their brains slowed down and even in some cases relaxed its hold completely.

Those, who meditated regularly, showed a remarkable change in the production of theta waves that were responsible for relaxation, calmness and contentment and of slowing down of alpha waves, which were responsible for the active conceptual and perceptual operations.

Richard Davidson at the University of Wisconsin at Madison conducted an in-depth study on the effects of meditation on the human personality by adding further credence to the meditation phenomenon. Davidson aimed his research on mapping changes in the brain due to the meditation practice. His studies indicated that meditation was conducive to changing activity from the prefrontal cortex to the left, leading to a more relaxed response to the stimuli. Furthermore, it revealed that regular practice of meditation could retrain the brain from the usual fight-flight response to that of understanding, accommodation and acceptance, which was a more relaxed response to the external world. This study offered credence to earlier studies done by Benson and Wallace during the 1970's, which had indicated that meditation produced a state of consciousness that was more relaxed and less combative as well as more peaceful and less aggressive.

> "A number of studies on yoga, meditation and breathing exercises are being conducted by researchers to reveal that their regular practice for a long time could have such beneficial consequences as reversing the build up of plaque that leads to the blockage of arteries; slowing down prostrate cancer; boosting the immune system of breast cancer patients; improving the condition of clinically depressed individuals and minimizing the therapeutic use of Viagra." (Ashok Malhotra: Paper on *Yoga Therapeutics*, 2007)

Other studies are being conducted on patients with heart problems. Deep breathing is used to slow down the oncoming of a heart attack. Even when the heart attack is happening and help is a few minutes away, deep breathing might be able to supply the needed oxygen to keep the person alive.

Moreover, certain *asanas* (physical postures) are being used to strengthen the lumber lordosis or the arch of the lower back. Regular practice of these postures is helpful in normalizing the lordosis curve, which in turn, leads to minimizing the stress on the lower back thus reducing the backache to a minimum. Some patients have practiced these *asanas* to get rid of the back pain permanently.

Other studies are being conducted to ascertain the curative value of regular practice of yoga postures, breathing and meditation exercises in connection with slowing down and reducing Diverticulitis and Diverticulosis, two major problems of the aging population.

Furthermore, yoga, meditation, and breathing exercises are being used in reducing and curing sleeplessness.

In addition, regular practice of yoga has been instrumental in reducing and even curing depression by increasing the level of neurotransmitters. {(GABA) Journal of Alternative and Complementary Medicine (Boston University Medical School)}

In her book on *Yoga for Depression*, Amy Weintraub discusses the root causes of depression, its manifestations and the methods of cure. She asserts that depression is due to the "over activation of the stress-response part and the under-activation of the well-being part of the nervous system."

She suggests three ways to fight depression: *medication, talk therapy* and *yoga. Medication* and *talk therapy* deal with depression at the chemical and social levels, whereas it is *yoga* that makes depression disappear like the heat of the sun that makes the water from the sidewalk to evaporate. According to *Yoga Philosophy,* we are the architects of our own life and happiness. Each moment is of utmost importance. Weintraub asserts that *yoga* offers us a philosophy of "Living Liberation," which is an antidote to depression. Depression consists of one's inability to be present to the experience of life." Those, who are depressed, live in the memories of the past and the hope of the future by missing the joys of the present moment. Weintraub asserts that yoga offers us *Jivanmukti* that is "self awake to this life." This is possible when we are present to our sensations, perceptions, feelings, emotions, images, ideas, breathing, sleeping, dreaming, etc. in this moment.

Though *yoga* practice is simple, it requires discipline, commitment and time. Medication, talk therapy and regular *yoga* practice of physical postures, breathing exercises and meditation would help restore the joys of life that were taken away by the depressive moods. According to Weintraub, recovery from depression requires a balance of medication, talk therapy and yoga.

Other studies at Vivekananda Yoga Research Foundation have found that regular practice of yoga and meditation by pregnant women improved birth rate and reduced instances of new babies being born prematurely. Daily practice of yoga brought significant changes in the reduction of "dry eye" effect and improved visual comfort in people, who spent a great deal of their time in front of computers (*Head and Face Medicine*). Practice of yoga and meditation was responsible for less soreness and injury among the athletes.

> "By putting credence into the findings of these researchers, some health insurance companies are encouraging their clients with heart problems to undertake the practice of meditation in order to avoid the occurrence of heart attacks in the future. More recently, studies are being conducted in Russia and the USA regarding the effects of breathing exercises and meditation on slowing down the heart rate and consumption of oxygen by the cosmonauts and astronauts, who are being trained for long exploratory flights to Mars, Mercury and other planets of our solar system. The hope is that through the practice of breathing and meditation techniques, the space-explorer-practioners will be able to slow down their metabolism to such a point that they will need less oxygen on a flight to these heavenly bodies, which might take three or more years. Though this interest of the scientists is laudable and the scientific research and its findings are impressive, all this exploration is nothing more than scratching the surface of this very complex phenomenon." (Malhotra: *Yoga Therapeutics*, 2007)

In spite of the studies cited here, research on meditation had merely been able to verify the scientifically measurable claims made by the practitioners. More recently, even though, some of the highly trained Buddhist monks have offered themselves as subjects for scientific research, where their states of meditation have been mapped and presented pictorially, most of the highly trained yoga meditators, Buddhist monks and Zen masters, who had declared that they possessed supernatural powers, had either not come forward or had not been approached by scientists in order that their esoteric powers be tested. Moreover, the current state of technology is inadequate to measure those complex levels of consciousness attained by masters of meditation. What of the yoga master who claimed he could materialize objects or could remember his previous lives; and of the T.M. pronouncement that its technique was uniquely suited to helping meditators acquire the power of levitation? Are we to disregard these assertions as fictional because they have yet to be substantiated scientifically? We should note that although the possibility exists that such claims might never come under scientific scrutiny, it is equally possible that future research might be able to scientifically demonstrate their truth or falsity.

Reports of Student Participants (1977)

The reports of meditators further corroborate the positive research findings. The following comments are from students who participated in an interdisciplinary and innovative course on "Creative Living: An Introduction to Yoga, Zen, and Mantra Meditation" offered for six weeks during the summer of 1977. Fifteen students met for 3 hours each day, four times a week, for six weeks. The first 2 hours were spent discussing the philosophy and method whereas the last hour was utilized in doing the yoga exercises and meditation techniques. Students were given 15 personality variables and were asked to keep a personal journal. Here they noted down the effects of yoga exercises and meditation on their personality after each class. At the end of six weeks of participation in the exercises and meditation, students reported their experiences. For the sake of confidentiality, the names of the students are changed and their reports are paraphrased.

Instant Nirvana

"Smith," 43 years of age, was married and had two children. He had resumed his studies after a break of almost fifteen years. He was quiet but extremely tense and nervous. After a six-week, sixty minutes a day session of yoga relaxation exercises and meditation practice, Smith reported the following:

Initially, I felt some embarrassment during the exercise and meditation phases of the course. I had the feeling that there was no fool like an old fool. But as the course progressed, I became more calm and collected. I also became more aware of things around me. One day following the meditation class I had to walk from the college campus to the Oneonta Nursing Home to pick up the car, a distance of about a mile. Usually, I would have walked briskly along to get there and cursed the fact that I had to do it. But on this day I strolled along leisurely and was aware of the various people, objects, trees, and scenery around me. I remembered thinking how the traffic did not seem as noisy as usual. When I arrived at the nursing home, I wasn't as tired as I would normally had been, and was somewhat sorry that I had to drive to go home. This awareness of my surroundings had steadily increased. I found that instead of becoming impatient waiting for the boss to arrive at the store in the morning, I sat and listened to the birds and watched the rays of the sun slip through the trees... I also found that I could accomplish much more at home with less effort and that I was more patient and understanding with my children. I was much more willing to listen to their ideas and not so fast to try to impose my desires on them. I found it easier to go to sleep at night and I felt more rested when I got up in the morning. I had also noted an increased openness to other people and I would listen to what they had to say without sticking my two cents worth in before

Ashok Kumar Malhotra

they were finished. Above all, there was an increasing ability to be alone with myself. When my wife was working and the children were out I did not have to turn the TV on for company.

"John," another student, reported changes in his personality:

> I feel a more effortless understanding of my work, especially in sculpture class, which I am taking simultaneously with this meditation course. When speaking to people I sense a greater understanding and I am able to eliminate much of the pettiness and frustrations. I feel more confident about my actions and am able to set my goals at a more obtainable level. Life seems fuller and I have a craving to savor it with more developed sensitivity.

> Lately, I have noticed more frustration in other people around me rather than in myself. That is a switch! Usually, I feel as if I have a million things to do, but my arms are tied behind me. Work, my creative ventures in the arts, are more humanistic, designed better, problems are solved a little faster and consequently smoothly and more effortlessly. In reference to sculpture, which I am working on this summer, I find that I can visually remember forms without a great deal of sketching, and the transitions between forms come much easier. Ideas come quickly and energy seems to be steady for getting the job done. I have grown in my awareness of the nature around me as I travel to and from school. The colors are richer and more vivid. I appreciate moments and cherish the moments I have with people. I enjoy now, rather than some idealistic venture in the future.

> I have been discovering that people are friendlier. My feelings are acceptable even anger. I make it a practice to share my feelings (of course in an en-

dearing fashion) with my wife and children. My feelings are more easily expressed and less controlled by thinking and judgments. Having developed some harmony within myself and knowing that I can freely express my emotions I am capable of being loved and to love....I am happy with meditation and feel it will get better in time (this Wednesday, I felt closest to a meditative state). I have my children doing the exercises with me, and they love to stand on their heads. Incidentally, they are better at the exercises than I. They are made of rubber.

Another participant in the meditation course was "Rob." He was thirty-four years old. He had returned to school because of two heart attacks, which precluded his continuing working at his trade. Rob had moved from the hectic and stressful life of Metropolitan Washington, D.C., to the peaceful rural countryside area of upstate New York. He was married and had two children. Rob was rather high-strung and found it difficult to relax. After a week of yoga meditation, Rob reported the following:

I slept well last night. This is not earth shattering, except as a rule I do not sleep well or soundly. The evenings on which my exercises were done, I slept soundly and awoke early and refreshed. Those evenings when exercises were not done, I slept poorly.

After two weeks of yoga and Zen meditation, Rob observed a significant drop in his blood pressure. He went for a routine check up at the hospital and his doctor was surprised to record 120/70 and 127/72 readings for Rob. He reported the following:

My historic norm for blood pressure is 135/85. In my doctor's office, I intentionally tried to relax and did so. When my cardiologist measured my blood pressure, it was 120/70. When I told him how I lowered my blood pressure he asked me to do it again. On the second reading the blood pressure was 127/72, still a significant drop. My doctor endorsed my continued practice of yoga and meditation as long as it did not severely tense my body.

Rob's wife, who had been deeply concerned with his health, made the following comments:

Rob does seem to sleep better and is calmer. He does need to meditate throughout the day in order to remain more calm. Another good effect is that he has lost a few pounds. I have not observed any negative effects so far.

"Jack," another student, reported the following changes after six weeks of continuous participation in the yoga exercises and meditation:

With the study of yoga I began to realize that many of my habits were mental modifications. The pleasurable effects of drinking alcohol and smoking hashish are certainly not natural. Ever since, I became aware of this, I have been able to curb my misuse of these substances tremendously. Now, I often turn down "getting high," in order to realize some "natural highs" from doing yoga exercises. Another improvement can be seen in the light of the mild depressions associated with poor performance in school. Since the beginning of the third week of the course, I have been much more motivated and involved in my school-work. In this manner I have developed new and involved deeper insights into my economics course, which I am taking along with this one. This certainly gives me the feeling of achievement and helps shun feelings of being an unorganized individual. Meditation has helped me develop spontaneity and expressiveness.

Jack also recorded a significant positive change in his interpersonal relationships.

Reports of Student Participants (2007)

During the past 30 years of teaching *Philosophy and Psychology of Yoga* to the undergraduate students, I have kept records of how the participants were affected by the worldview as well as the experiential technique of yoga. The reports listed below are from a randomly chosen sample. The students followed a fairly simple course format. Between 30-35 students met on each Wednesday for two and one half hours for a span of fourteen weeks. During the first one and half hours, we discussed the philosophy and method of yoga whereas the last hour was spent on doing physical, breathing, meditation as well as systematic relaxation and visualization exercises. On the first day of class, students were given 15 personality variables consisting of self-concept, self-confidence, self-love, love for others, self-discipline, friendliness, enjoyment, contentment, repulsion, hatred, anger, anxiety, fear of death, reflection and meaning of life. The variables were selected from Personal Orientation Inventory as well as from Patanjali's Yoga Sutras.

On the first day of class, students were asked to complete a form rating these 15 variables from 1 to 5 where 1 was the weakest and 5 the strongest. Moreover, each student was asked to keep a personal journal to note down on a weekly basis any change occurring due to the study of the yoga philosophy as well as the practice of the technique. In their personal journal, students were advised to describe this change in an honest manner without dramatization or exaggeration. At the end of

14 weeks, a two-page long essay summarizing the effects of the philosophy and technique of yoga on the student's personality was submitted for grade and evaluation.

For the sake of confidentiality, the names of the students are changed and their reports are paraphrased.

"Henry" dubbed himself as a negative person with little regard for himself or others. He characterized his stance on the world as angry, impatient and anxious. Encountering strangers made him nervous and especially when they asked questions, he went in a state of panic. He designated his personality as sluggish, inertial and lazy lacking all inner motivation. He felt like a cloud wandering aimlessly in the firmament. Moreover, Henry was accustomed to shutting off emotions towards disease, decay and death.

After attending the first yoga class, as he started writing his journal, he became aware of his "good for nothing" behavior. This initial attempt at reflection about himself clarified for him the challenge he was facing about his own personality. After a few weeks of the study of yoga philosophy and the practice of the physical and breathing exercises, Henry felt that he had more energy in the body and enhanced clarity of mind. He could deal with his schoolwork and family issues with more calm and clarity. As the semester progressed, his self-confidence improved, his energy level was amplified, and at times he felt like a 'daredevil' who could do anything. Though he had kept his emotions under control when his beloved grandmother was hospitalized, Henry had to meet the challenge head-on when he learned about her death. Instead of being shattered by the news, he found his private time to mourn her loss in his own way. Through constant reflection on the meaning of life and death, he kept on doing his daily chores without being hampered by this great loss. The yogic exercises and the study of its philosophy helped Henry to take notice of the world around with much more intensity. Overall, Henry felt that these fourteen weeks of indulgence in yoga and meditation transformed him into a better and more matured person, who now was in an improved position to take charge of his life and destiny.

Another participant was "Nancy." She designated herself as an extremely stressed out person. Though she found vigorous exercise as an anti-dote to her stress, it did not reduce it completely. As Nancy participated in the class, she was drawn towards *pranayama* or the breathing exercises. Breathing component of the yoga technique worked wonders for her. When she felt the onset of anxiety that was going to stress her out, Nancy practiced the inhalation, retention and exhalation aspects of the technique that helped her to take control of herself. With regular practice of this breathing routine, she was able to ward off the anxiety fit and instead was able to generate a feeling of well being, which previously might have been a rare experience for her. With a regular dosage of breathing regulation, Nancy was able to develop more self-confidence that in turn enhanced her enjoyment of daily activities, which further lead to being more tolerant and friendly towards others. She adopted a calmer and less hostile approach when she encountered other people. As she was more comfortable with herself, others felt the same towards her.

The biggest bonus of practicing the breathing technique was dealing with the chronic problem of sleeplessness. She had hard time falling asleep. Along with breathing exercises, Nancy tried the yoga technique of systematic relaxation of the muscles of the body that lead to a very restful sleep. On waking the next day, she felt less tired and had an abundance of energy. An added benefit of learning about the yoga worldview of the interconnection between human beings and their environment lead Nancy to improving her dietary habits thus culminating in improved personal health and well being.

"Lola" was another participant, who regarded herself as an "A" type personality because she had many irons in the fire. She was always full of pep and energy and believed that she could do a number of things at the same time. Though she was a dancer, who had previously taken a few lessons in yoga techniques and martial arts, she was easily distracted by the exuberance of energy that was constantly overflowing her personality's banks. During the course of the semester, as she studied the philosophy and the technique of yoga, she learned the importance of the central theme, which was to become one-pointed in her daily activities. Instead of being pulled by diverse projects, which fascinated her equally, she learned to pick one and put her heart and soul into it by offering her dedicated engagement. By concentrating on one task, she could get the maximum joy out of it. This way of focusing on a single task, where her entire being was fully engrossed without any distractions, converted the ordinary into an extra-ordinary moment that was experienced in the most intense way. Doing one activity with full attention and dedication brought about immense joy, contentment and relaxation.

"David," another participant reported the following changes: Along with my course on Philosophy and Psychology of Yoga, David took another course on Yoga and Health. This second course focused on different physical postures and their health benefits. He learned the philosophy, psychology, science, history and methodology of the ancient *Yoga* system in my course. Since the two courses complemented each other, David practiced physical, breathing and meditation exercises three times a week throughout the semester. He reported many fruitful results.

The philosophical world-view of *Yoga* as presented in the Patanjali's *Yoga Sutras* and its scientific method were very helpful in grasping the holistic nature of the discipline. He found out that *Yoga* was not just limited to a set of physical exercises but was a complete system catering to the improvement of the whole person.

David reported that the physical exercises were catalytic towards his "improved balance, flexibility and pliability." They contributed immensely towards his improvement in basketball game, rock climbing, running and hiking and karate technique. Moreover, he noticed that he had fewer bouts with illness and injuries during the course of the semester. In the past, he used to suffer from a chronic problem with stuffy nose and had hard time breathing. The practice of *pranayama* or breathing exercises on a regular basis cleared up the sinus problem completely. The physical and meditation exercises done during the class relaxed him to such a point that he felt a complete relief from the congestion and stress associated with it. He realized that these problems were psychosomatic and the practice of yoga on a regular basis uprooted them. David, who practiced yoga by himself without being part of a group, learned a number of other lessons from the yoga training, which he outlined as: "be here now," "helpfulness towards others," "becoming a better person," "being friendlier and loving towards others." Overall, the yoga class and practice helped David obtain a better understanding of his inner capacities and his self.

The eight students whose reports are presented here were among more than 60, who reported on the effects of yoga philosophy and meditation exercises. Our research that was done during 1977 was repeated during 2007 and the results were almost identical.

A majority of students reported that their self-concept, self-confidence, self-love, love for others, self-discipline, friendliness, enjoyment and contentment improved significantly. This was noticeable in their daily encounters with people within their circles of friendship as well as with their encounters with strangers. On the other hand, their propensity towards repulsion, hatred, anger, anxiety, fear of death, and meaninglessness were depleted to such a point that they started enjoying the wondrous gift of life.

No student reported any negative effect from the practice of the physical postures, breathing exercises or the meditative practice.

While the reader might be tempted to challenge the validity of these self-reports as a reliable means of measuring changes in personality, s/he should be aware of the state of purely scientific research in this area. At present, hardheaded empirical investigations in this domain of personality are still minimal, and perhaps by themselves, could not offer us full insight into this subjective realm of human experience. In our study, the subject was not reduced to an object, but retained his subjectivity and participated in the research as a co-investigator. The subject was not passive, but was actively involved in monitoring changes, which were taking place within him. Furthermore, the subject was uniquely qualified to assume this role, for s/he had immediate access to the inner self, and could provide the deepest insight into changes in personality affected by meditation.

Personal Reflections

Ours is an extremely stressful society. A number of diseases or illnesses are associated with the people's ability or inability to cope with stress. Studies by Bernie Siegel, Carl Simonton, Hans Selye and others have indicated a clear correlation between stress and such diseases as cancer, depression and sexual dysfunction.

Regular practice of yoga and meditation does influence the body and brain of the meditator by improving the total health of the person. The studies done by the above researchers indicate that regular meditation and visualization resulted in boosting the immune system of women with different stages of breast cancer. Women who actively participated in yoga exercises by making them as part of their daily routine and meditated on a regular basis were able to increase their white cells to fight the cancerous growth.

I have a personal experience dealing with this tragic disease. My wife had gone for a regular medical check up and found out that she had breast cancer, which had metastasized. The doctors gave her 6 months to a year to live. Since both of us believed that yoga, meditation and visualization would help meet this challenge, we worked together as a team and followed the routine with full faith, which lead to a miracle where my wife survived the cancer for five years.

I do believe and my conviction is attested by my own studies that meditation and yoga lead to many beneficial effects on the human personality. I have practiced yoga and meditation for more than 30 years and still feel as young and energetic as I was when I was in my twenties." (Malhotra: *Yoga Therapeutics*, 2007)

Here is a personal instance worthy of mention that had transformed my daily life from living in excruciating pain to a manageable/normal life.

While I was a college student in India, a yoga master trained me for five years. However, when I arrived in the USA to pursue my graduate studies, I was sporadic in my practice of yoga. Almost 30 years ago, while I was in the process of renovating the attic of my house, an incident happened that opened my eyes to the art of yoga that I had neglected for a number of years.

I was in my middle thirties. Since I possessed excellent health, I used to believe that I could do anything by myself provided that I put my heart to it. While fixing the attic, I had assigned to myself the task of carrying thirty two pieces of sheet rock from the truck to the third floor while passing through two narrow staircases. Driven by the "dare devilish spirit," I told myself that I did not need anyone else's help to carry these sheet rocks to the attic. It was the month of July when the temperature in the attic was more than 105 degrees. As I struggled singly with twisting and turning each sheet rock through these narrow staircases, I also was twisting and turning my upper and lower back. After carrying the first 31 sheet rocks, I was totally exhausted. Though my entire body was complaining, my mind was dictating to me to carry the last one to finish the work. As I did not listen to the appeal of my body, and when I was in the middle of the second staircase with a twisted sheet rock and a twisted body, I heard a crackling sound that sent pangs of excruciating pain through my back and legs. I felt that my body above the hips was going to crumble down like the building that was dynamited. A blood curdling sound of pain rushed out of my body that caught the attention of my wife who came to my rescue. As she helped to pull the sheet rock up the steps and placed it flat on the attic floor, I fell down on the ground with another cry of pain. I lay down in the hallway floor for a few moments to collect my senses. The pain was so intense that I felt that I was going to pass out. My wife brought me a glass of water. I took a few sips that helped me to stay conscious.

As I was lying there I thought of the yoga exercises that were taught by my teacher a decade ago. I remembered him saying to us that the lower back pain was the result of bad posture or poor lifting habits. "You must avoid this at all cost," was the sound of his voice echoing through my ears. Moreover, he had told us that if we did not listen to his first advise and messed ourselves up, there was a second advise that would rectify the situation. It consisted of maintaining one's lumber lordosis i.e. the curve formed by the hips and the shoulders as one would lie on one's back.

Here I was flat on the ground and in great pain. In order to sit up, I needed to do something to get a relief from this discomfort. I tried to press gently on my hips and shoulders to form the arch of the lumber lordosis. Though it felt horribly sore, it eased the pressure on the back. I maintained this arch for a count of ten and then released the tension by gently pushing the lower back against the carpeted floor. Immediately, I felt a great relief from the tenderness caused by the twisting and turning of the tendons of the lower back. I repeated this exercise five more times and to my surprise, I could get up without feeling any more pain.

The next day I got an appointment with the doctor, who took X-Rays and found that one of those five vertebrae composing the lumber of my backbone was cracked during my childhood years. Since no one treated it, it got repaired by itself but was out of alignment. Every time, when I would lift anything, the stress on these vertebrae could cause the excruciating pain that I had undergone a day before. Since my lifting of sheet rock had made it tender again, it would be acting up throughout my life. That meant that I would have to live with a chronic lower backache. The doctor prescribed ibuprofens as the pain reliever whereas I tried alternative therapies offered by the chiropractics, acupuncture and acupressure. After trying these treatments for a few months, I was disappointed. They were not focusing on the healing of the lower back whereas the yoga exercises for the lumber lordosis zeroed in on the lower back like the nano-tubes that went directly to the sore spot where the ailment resided. I have been practicing these yogic exercises continuously for the past thirty years. They have made my lower back so functional that I have played tennis on a regular basis and have done an outstanding job by playing against much younger players. This is all due to the yoga exercises and an optimistic outlook on life.

During the past 30 years, my students, who had practiced yoga continuously for a long time, had told me similar stories of the positive effects of yoga and meditation on their physical and emotional health, social interaction and spiritual development. I have cited a sample of these reflections of my students in the previous section.

"At present there are close to 15 million Americans doing some form of yoga and meditation on a regular basis using physical exercises for toning up their bodies, breathing exercises for emotional balance and meditation for reducing stress of the mind and gaining spiritual control. The scientific research on the healing potential of yoga and mediation has contributed much to the popularity of this ancient discipline.

When something works for our stress-ridden society and also makes people feel good, they go all out to try it at least once. This kind of attitude of the people had made meditation as an all-pervasive tool, which at the present time, is being used in the hospitals, schools, law firms, government buildings, prisons, police stations, sports arenas and even in the film studios. Moreover, special rooms are set-aside for meditation at the hospitals, airports and churches.

It could be argued that the interest in yoga and meditation is a passing fit, which is transient and going to evaporate with the heat of future scientific research. But so far, it seems to be standing on its own firm footing because of the support provided by the scientific research of the past thirty years. If the research continues with the same gusto and the scientists keep coming up with more positive findings, people will indulge in this holistic discipline by delving deeper into its theory and practice. This serious indulgence might help the human race to enjoy a healthy life in the future." (Malhotra: *Yoga Therapeutics, 2007*)

Evaluative Comments

Although research on the effects of meditation on the human personality had been moving at a slow pace during the 1970's and 1980's, it had picked up much more speed from 1990 to 2007. By using technology (e.g., Electroencephalogram) and psychological instruments (e.g., Personal Orientation Inventory or POI) during the 1990's and more recently, by using MRI and other techniques to map the intricate changes, science is able to measure a number of significant physical and psychological alterations resulting from meditation. All this has offered much credence to the reports made by the practioners of meditations. However, since the human personality is a complex network of physical, emotional, intellectual, and behavioral elements, science with its entire armamentarium may not by itself be capable of providing all the information about the deepest aspects of human consciousness. So far scientific studies have been limited to investigating merely the periphery of the realm of human consciousness. To obtain a wider view, the empirical approach of the sciences needs to be complemented by the humanistic approach, which utilizes the resources of the human subjects being investigated (as we did by presenting the self-reports of students who participated in courses on meditation). This humanistic approach treats the subjects as co-researchers in the investigation rather than as mere guinea pigs. The empirical approach is limited because it informs us only about variables measurable by scientific instruments and is less capable in measuring what is valuable or significant to the individual. Thus, the blending of the two methods can give us a more comprehensive profile of the human personality.

One further point needs to be made. Since we assumed the complex nature of the relationship between meditation and personality, we believe that no one perspective popular, scientific, or humanistic by itself, can fully enlighten us about the nature of this relationship. But when looked at together and synthesized, these perspectives can offer us a more holistic view. In order to obtain this comprehensive view, we have adopted a phenomenological approach, which consisted first, in describing each perspective (philosophical, scientific, or humanistic) as impartially as possible, second, in remaining neutral in our judgment by not pitching one perspective against the other or by not regarding one perspective as superior to the other in terms of its nearness to truth, and third, by attempting to bring out (wherever possible) the complementarity of these perspectives.

PART IV

Encounters with Gurus and Practitioners

Ashok Kumar Malhotra

Baba Muktananda
and
The Siddha Yoga

Baba Muktananda was the head of the Gurudev Siddha Peeth in Ganeshpuri, India. He came from a tradition of teachers who were known for transmitting spiritual power directly to their students. This passing of spiritual energy or enlightenment from the teacher to the disciple was called *shaktipat*. Muktananda received his *shaktipat* from his guru Nityananda. From that day onward, Muktananda became a fully awakened spiritual being who could impart this same power to anyone through his look, touch, or word. Muktananda's spiritual activities were confined to India till 1970. On the invitation of his Western disciples, Muktananda took a spiritual tour of the United States to check the feasibility of setting up a branch of his institute. Since the tour was highly successful, his disciples started the Siddha Yoga Center near Liberty, New York, during the early nineteen seventies. Muknananda attracted disciples from all strata of life. Intellectuals, professionals, students, business people, and those who were looking for a quick spiritual-high, flocked to his Siddha Yoga Center. Muktananda was affectionately called "Baba" by his disciples.

During the late seventies and early eighties I visited the Center a couple of times with my students. Baba was glad to see our group. At different times, he talked to some of them and gave them Indian names, which delighted the students. Since I liked the way my students were treated at the Siddha Yoga Center, I requested the

Center staff for an interview with the Baba. The interview was readily arranged.

The interview was set at 9 a.m. Since I lived in Oneonta and the drive to the town of Liberty took two hours, I had to get up at 5 a.m. to make it to the interview. As I arrived at the Siddha Yoga Center at 8:30 a.m., I was greeted by one of the disciples. Since everything had been arranged, I was ushered to a room where a small carpet had been laid out. A young beautiful woman, who was the Baba's interpreter, took me into the room and asked me to sit down. While I waited for the Baba, she and I exchanged some pleasantries. She was a bright charming woman who was dedicated to the Baba and to the work of the Center. She told me that Baba felt much more comfortable speaking in Hindi than in English and if it was all right with me she would be the interpreter. I was happy to know that she was willing to assist me but in reality I did not need her help because Hindi was my mother tongue. I told her that though I did not need the services of a translator, it would be wonderful to have her present during the interview.

Just then I heard the door open and Baba Muktananda appeared. To greet him, I stood up and with both hands folded I said "namaste" in Hindi, which was an Indian greeting. Baba returned my greeting with his folded hands and asked me to sit down. As I sat down a few feet across from him, I observed him carefully. He was a fine looking man with a powerful gaze. My mind sent the message that the secret of Baba's enlightenment was sitting just behind those two powerful eyes.

To make me feel relaxed, Baba said:

"I am so happy that you are able to come. In the past you had brought your students with you. They are so young and impressionable. They seemed eager to learn about the spiritual life of India."

Ashok: "Baba, I am delighted that you have given me this personal audience despite the demands on your time put by your disciples."

Baba: "Since you have been a regular visitor of our Center, I like you and your students. You must have some questions to ask. Please proceed."

Ashok: "Baba, I teach Indian philosophy and religion at the State University of New York at Oneonta. At present, I am teaching a course on yoga, meditation, and recent Hindu religious groups in America. Included in our discussion is the emergent Asian religious phenomenon. Since there are so many people who are claiming to be gurus or enlightened teachers, it is very hard for an ordinary person to separate authentic from inauthentic gurus. What criteria should an ordinary person use to assess who is a genuine guru and who is not?"

After giving a hearty laugh at my simple question, Baba said:

"People ask me this question all the time and I don't blame them a bit. There is a proliferation of self-appointed gurus. Some of them are genuine whereas others are hoaxes. People have to become very discerning these days. They have to read up on the writings of these self-proclaimed prophets. My answer to your question is simple. If you are in search of a genuine guru, you have to prepare yourself. Preparation is hard and requires a great deal of time and genuine effort. When you have prepared yourself, the guru will appear or you will find one. But don't be in a hurry. Because in your haste you may find what you deserve."

Ashok: "What do you mean by this statement?"

Baba: "My message is simple. If you are a stupid person, you will find a stupid guru and if you are a bright person, you will find an intelligent guru. One gets the guru one deserves."

Ashok: "I will convey this answer to my students. They will be happy to know what you have said. Can you tell me what shaktipat is and how one can obtain it?"

Baba: "*Shaktipat* is the way through which an enlightened master passes part of his enlightenment to his disciple through touch, look, or word. It can be imparted by a guru who has achieved enlightenment through his own endeavors or has obtained it through his guru."

Ashok: "Did you obtain your enlightenment through your own efforts or through your Guru's help?"

Baba: "I prepared myself through reading the scriptures, by doing meditation, and by living the life, which imbibed the life of my guru, Nityananda. When my guru found me ready for enlightenment, he gave me the *shaktipat*."

Ashok: "Since you obtained your enlightenment through your own efforts and through the *shaktipat*, you can be called a *siddha*."

Baba: "These are different words for the same thing."

Ashok: "You can pass this enlightenment to others, I am told."

Baba: "Yes, I can. That is why we conduct the weekend spiritual sessions called the 'Gateway to the self,' where I impart *shaktipat* to a person from the audience."

Ashok: "Baba, how do you decide who should be the recipient of your *shaktipat*?"

Baba: "I have the intuitive sense to know from the face of a person whether he had prepared himself for the enlightened touch."

Ashok: "Why do Americans of all walks of life flock to these spiritual centers?"

Baba: "Americans are crazy people. They are looking for a quick fix for the emptiness they feel within. They are accustomed to working hard at their jobs but have no patience in dealing with the real problems of life. They have not been taught to face the emptiness of their existence. They believe that everything can be bought through money and that is their biggest problem."

Ashok: "How are you providing them with a solution?"

Baba: "Our center is like a pseudo-therapy clinic. Since the American society is a big factory that turns out many crazy people, who are not willing to work hard at understanding their existential predicament or look down upon getting help from a therapist, they come to us. We provide them the pseudo-therapy in the garb of spirituality."

Ashok Kumar Malhotra

Ashok: "You have been wonderful to me by first consenting to give this interview and then spending time to answer my questions."

Baba: "I like you and have something special to give you this weekend."

Ashok: "What is going on this weekend?"

Baba: "You are very lucky that during this weekend I will be here to conduct the 'Gateway to the Self' session. If you join us you might get a special treat from me."

Ashok: "What will that be?"

Baba: "You have to guess!"

Just at that point the beautiful and charming lady interpreter interrupted us by saying that Baba had other appointments and, therefore, the interview was over. I thanked the Baba for his graciousness in dealing with my questions. I told him that I was lucky to have spent those thirty minutes with him. Baba folded his hands and said Namaste. Before leaving the room, he reminded me of the most significant weekend of my life, which awaited me.

As I came out of the room, a bunch of the Baba's regular disciples were waiting to hear from me about the interview. One of them asked me if the Baba had said something very special to me. I replied that the Baba wanted me to join the "Gateway to the Self" session this weekend because he planned to give me something most significant. As all of those disciples were looking at me with hungry eyes, they said in one voice: "Of course you are coming to the session this weekend!"

I told them that I had not made up my mind. They were surprised at my response and told me that I was making a mistake by not taking this open invitation to be certainly enlightened. My response was that I would think about it during the next two days to decide whether the enlightenment was worth $350, which was the price of the weekend session. As I left the building, the disciples were in a state of disbelief that I did not take the Baba Muktananda's offer of enlightenment.

Though I had not given up trying to prepare for enlightenment, I did not think I was ready yet or, most probably, I hadn't found the right master yet.

Swami Rama
and
The Himalayan Institute

Swami Rama was the founder of the Himalayan Institute and the Himalayan Institute Hospital Trust in India. In 1970, he served as a research subject for the Menninger Foundation Research Project on Voluntary Control of Internal States. Under the laboratory conditions, he was able to move a needle from a distance, which offered credence to the claim that the mind could control the body at will. This revolutionized the scientific research in the area of autonomic functioning and the human ability to control the body.

Our group of 11 SUNY students and two professors got up very early in order to be ready to go to the Ashram to meet the famous Swami Rama. The Ashram was located on the Ganges River in the sacred town of

Ashok Kumar Malhotra

Rishikesh in India. The Beatles had followed the Maharishi to this same town during the sixties to obtain personal mantras to keep their unity and sanity intact. Every member of our group was excited to encounter this sage of the Himalayas. We arrived at the Ashram at 9 a.m. We were welcomed at the gate by two young American disciples. Since they had been expecting us, we were immediately ushered into the visitor's tent surrounded by a beautifully laid out garden next to the river. At 9:30 a.m. we were greeted by a woman guru who led a meditation session for the group. She was a soft-spoken, black woman from the USA who conducted the session with ease and grace. At 11 a.m., Dr. Usharbudh Arya, director of the meditation center at Minneapolis, introduced himself and asked the group to raise questions on any topic of their choice. Students asked him a number of questions on meditation, the use of a mantra, and the nature of the monastic life. Dr. Arya spoke for 30 minutes and presented a scholarly discussion on these topics.

At 11:30 a.m., Swami Rama came in and sat down in front of the group on a raised platform, which was specially prepared for big gatherings. He had a terrific presence. The first thing he did was to ask whether everyone in the group had something to eat. Then he directed his gentle and charismatic gaze toward the group and asked me to describe the goals of the SUNY program in India. After giving him a quick summary highlight of the program, the following conversation took place:

Swami: "I have something special to give to the group, which I will reveal later. What do you want me to do for you?"

(This kind of introduction put everyone in the group at ease.)

Ashok: "How do you choose a guru? What kind of discernment is needed?"

Swami: "You do not need to choose a guru. When the disciple is ready, the guru appears. The disciple must prepare the ground so that the guru can be born. A guru is not just a person from outside, it could be you from within. A guru resides in you. It is you in the inner core of your being. Why look around for it outside yourself?"

Ashok: "Who is a swami? What requirements have to be fulfilled to become a swami?"

Swami: "A swami is a person who has developed self-control. A person accomplishes it through discarding attachments to name, fame, and fortune. Furthermore, a swami detaches himself from the family, friends, and the material world. This does not mean that a swami refuses to live in the world, he does. He is of this world but has a full command of his senses and the ego. He has learned the art of body-mind control and detachment."

Ashok: "How ought one to live in this world, which constantly invokes in us unlimited desires?"

Ashok Kumar Malhotra

Swami: "A person's life is a 'yatra' or a 'journey.' This journey ought to be undertaken so as to experience the divine spark within before the journey is over. But how can one accomplish that? What attitudes need to be inculcated? Bounded by time, this journey is very short and limited. As one of the Indian folk poets has said: 'Walk through life by taking delight in everything but do not get attached to anything.' Get involved in an action. Let your mind and body be engrossed in it, enjoy it, but be totally detached from it. Do not get stuck in the world!"

Ashok: "We have heard that you sleep very little, that is only two and one-half hours each day for the past forty years. How do you manage it while being so creative and alert?"

Swami: "I have trained myself to go to sleep only for two and one-half hours each day. When I sleep, I have a deep sleep, a dreamless sleep. During my sleep, I regenerate my physical and spiritual batteries. I also meditate a great deal during the day and the night. Since meditation is alert sleep, it is a substitute for sleep. During meditation, my mind is fully alert. I do not do anything but am a mere witness. I observe myself sleep. I

watch myself relax. All this gives me
a great deal of energy and vigor."

After answering these questions, Swami Rama told the audience that he had decided to give the SUNY group a wonderful gift — the gift of a title to their professor. He then directed his compassionate gaze toward me and with his spiritual authority he assigned to me the title of "Swami Rishikeshananda," which meant that from that day onward I should be regarded as the Swami, who was the joy of Rishikesh. On hearing this utterance from their revered Guru, the disciples of Swami Rama gazed at me with hungry eyes and envious faces, indicating to me that I must have done something extremely good in my past life to be bestowed upon such a spiritual honor.

Guru Maharajji
and
The Divine Light Mission

The Divine Light Mission was introduced into the USA in 1971 by a teenager from India called Guru Maharajji. When his father died, the eight year old Guru Maharajji was appointed to head the Mission and to spread the spiritual message to the West.

As the teenage Guru arrived in the USA, he attracted such followers as the rock music groupies, the academic dropouts, the organic food lovers, the flower children, and the alienated youths. The most famous convert to the Mission was Rennie Davis of the Chicago Seven anti-Vietnam war protestors. Within a few years of its introduction to the USA, the Divine Light Mission amassed a great deal of fortune through operating lucrative businesses as well as generous donations from the devotees.

Though I read many newspaper and magazine reports on Guru Maharajji and the speed with which his movement had spread in the USA, I never had any personal encounters with the Guru. One of my students, however, reported the following story:

> Guru Maharajji, who had declared himself to be the perfect master, the incarnation for this generation of the primordial vibration of the universe, the quintessence of the past messiahs, and the God-incarnate, was giving a speech at a five star hotel. Among a host of others, a young reporter from a small mid-western newspaper was there to cover the event. Since he was new to the job, he wanted to make a big splash by doing something unusual for his newspaper. After giving his customary kind of speech that involved a few polemically tainted anecdotes and parables, which invoked a great deal of laughter, he reiterated his status as the Child-God who was the last savior of mankind.

> After listening to the speech of Guru Maharajji, the young reporter went in front of the stage and threw a lemon custard pie on the Guru's face and rushed out of the lecture hall. He hastened up to his hotel room, sat down at his desk, and wrote down on his writing pad: "Today I Threw a Lemon Custard Pie on the God's Face."

> While he was writing these lines, he was so excited at this extraordinary deed that his heart was racing a mile a second. Just then there was a knock at his door. As he hastened to open the door, he saw a strange sight. Two angelic guards of the Guru had followed him to his room. To teach him a lesson

about his horrendously sacrilegious act, the two angels beat him to a pulp to teach him once and for all time that the Guru can give you instant nirvana, when you please him but instant hell if you displease him.

Bhaktivedanta Prabhupada
and
The Hare Krishna Movement

The Hare Krishna Movement was started by Bhaktivedanta Prabhupada, a Hindu Guru from India. He came to the United States during the sixties to spread the message of Lord Krishna. His exotic dress, sensuous music, and dancing attracted a number of disciples who were dropouts from the drug culture of the sixties.

I never met Bhaktivedanta in person but had a few scuffles with his devotees. In 1980, I was taking a group of students to India for a SUNY Study Abroad Program. As I met with the SUNY group at the JFK Airport in New York, the check in went very smoothly. We collected our boarding passes and bee lined toward the departure gate. While we were waiting at the gate, a few concerned parents of the students were going through the usual hugging, kissing, and goodbye routine. My job was to offer assurance to the parents that their children would be taken care of in India.

An extremely nervous father of a female student came to me with a shaky voice and said: "Professor, say something which can give me the assurance that my little daughter will be safe in India." He insisted that I should say it quickly in the fewest possible words. I put my hand on his shoulder and replied: "Listen, my friend, the one thing on which I have edge over you is that I am a native of India, who understands the culture and speaks four of its languages. Your daughter will be safer with me than you." On hearing my reply, the father felt relieved and bid farewell to his daughter. While this drama was going on with the father and me, I was suddenly pulled over by a guy with a shaven head and who was attired in an ochre robe. He must have been in his twenties. He handed me a copy of the *Bhagavad Gita As It Is*. He told me that I should revere it rest of my life because it was coming directly from the founder of the faith, Bhaktivedanta Prabhupada. Since I was in a hurry to take the plane, I quickly looked at the book and immediately handed it back to him with the remark that I already had a copy of the same translation. The guy in the ochre robe insisted that I take this copy with me into the plane because it was the most recent edition and was personally blessed by the Guru. And, furthermore, if I took this gift from him, my journey would be successful. I insisted that it was redundant to have a second copy of the book, which I already possessed. I suggested that he should give this book to someone who could put it to a better use. He said with impatience, "Carry it in the plane. This will be the best company for anyone because the *Bhagavad Gita* is Krishna's word. When you read the book, you are listening to the God Krishna. What else could be better company? Nothing else in the world was as important as the words of Krishna, the hero of the *Bhagavad Gita*."

I told him again that I did not want to buy another copy of the book. To which he responded: "This book is a gift for you. Take it and enjoy it." As I was in a hurry and wanted to get away from him, I took the book from him and was almost ready to go through the security gate, the man in the ochre robe stopped me. He insisted that I should give him a donation for the book. I told him that I did not have to give him anything because the book was a gift from him. On hearing these words, his face changed from being friendly to being greedy. He said to me in his stern voice that the donation was $25. "Take the book and leave $25 or you can't have the book." I got irritated at this episode and threw the book back into his hands and told him that he was doing a disservice to the Krishna name and the Hare Krishna Movement. As I left the book with him, he shouted at me by saying that he was doing nothing but service to God Krishna. At that moment, I did not care what he said because I was in hurry to take the plane and get everyone in my group to be comfortably seated.

After getting through the security, I met with my fifteen students. I almost forgot the episode. The flight was more than 18 hours long and was extremely tiring. As we were landing in New Delhi, we were anxious to get out. After going through the immigration formalities, we were ready to go outside to inhale some fresh air. After picking up our luggage, I assembled the group and we marched out of the airport into the land of India. One of my students commented that it was very exciting to step foot in this ancient land. He could not believe that he was actually there in the land of Mahatma Gandhi and Nehru.

Since our travel agent was waiting for us outside the gate, we started looking for him. The outside was as crowded as the inside of the airport. People were jamming up every bit of space and were staring at passengers. The taxi drivers, tour guides, and relatives of passengers had taken over every inch of the space. After wading through the crowd, I had a glimpse of the travel agent, who was standing behind rows of people. He waved at me and I acknowledged him with my waving of the hand. He pushed people in front of him so that he could get to our group. As we tried to move forward by pushing the crowd, we were able to come to an open space. Just then my JFK nightmare was repeated. There stood a bunch of Hare Krishna Kids dressed up in ochre robes holding the *Bhagavad Gita* in their hands. As they saw me with a bunch of American students, they pounced upon us as hungry vultures. One of them rushed in my direction while waving the *Bhagavad Gita As It Is* at us. He tried to forcibly push the book into my hands. The man who forced the book in my hand looked just like the one I had left behind in New York. Before he could land the book into my hands, I told him that I was tired and upset, and therefore he should leave me alone. The devotee in the ochre robe saw anxiety and anger written all over my face and said: "You are the best candidate for the *Bhagavad Gita*. It will relax you and take away all your fears and troubles. I will give you this special volume free though others have to make a donation." While he was rambling on with his usual speech, I had reached the travel agent to whom I made a request that he should get this bugger off my back. The travel agent looked at the man in the ochre robe and said to him in Hindi that if he did not leave his group alone he would be thrown to the dogs and be eaten alive, which would be the quickest way for him to join God Krishna in heaven. Though these words scared some of the Hare Krishna devotees, the others followed us to our bus pleading to take copies of the book on our journey to the hotel. As one of our students took the book, the man in the ochre robe insisted that the student should give him 250 rupees as donation. On hearing the word donation, the student threw the book back into the hands of the man in the ochre robe while the bus sped away in the direction of the hotel.

Maharishi Mahesh Yogi and Transcendental Meditation (T.M.)

During the 1970's, there was a great deal of interest in yoga and meditation. This was due to the claims made by the proponents of T.M. that it had the formula to offer practitioners instant Nirvana. I had read about these claims in journals, magazines, and had encountered a number of followers of the T.M. movement. The information gathered from these sources seemed to be impressive. Since it was such a hot topic, students asked me to create a summer course called, "Creative Living through Yoga, Zen and T.M." Being guided by the students' enthusiasm and my own research interest in the subject, I went ahead and created the course, which was accepted by the college.

The summer school catalog advertised the course with the above title. A week before the course was to be taught I received a registered letter from the lawyer representing T.M. in California. The long drawn out legal letter threatened to sue me and the college for using the word T.M. in the title of my course. The explanation given in the letter indicated that since T.M. was a registered trade mark, no one was permitted to teach it unless the individual was duly trained by the Maharishi himself. At the bottom of the letter, I was told that I should get in touch with the local T.M. representative to give him assurance that the word T.M. would be stricken from the title of my course. If I did not abide by the warning and proceeded to teach the course as advertised, I could be brought to court and sued.

This news perplexed me. I called up the local T.M representative who had already received a copy of the letter. I asked him to come to my house where we could talk this matter over a cup of tea.

The T.M. representative came over immediately. He was a young man in his mid-twenties. I offered him tea to which he consented. I asked him if the lawyers of the T.M. were serious about suing me for using the word T.M. in the title of my course. He emphatically told me that it was a serious matter and I should listen to their advice. The following conversation took place between the two of us:

Ashok: "Why can't I use the word T.M. in the title of my course?"

Rep.: "T.M. is a registered trademark, which can be used only by a teacher of T.M. who is trained by the Maharishi himself."

Ashok: "I have a Ph.D. in philosophy and have been trained in yoga and meditation by a Hindu yogi. I have also taught yoga to undergraduate students for five years. I have given lectures on yoga to various national and international groups. Does not that qualify me to discuss T.M.?"

Rep.: "But you were never taught by the Maharishi in the technique of T.M."

Ashok: "I have read the Maharishi's translation of the *Bhagavad Gita* and his book on *Creative Intelligence*. Furthermore, I have read the texts of his various speeches and have watched his interviews on TV. His method of T.M. is nothing more than the mantra method discussed in the *Yogasutras* of Patanjali and the *Bhagavad Gita* of Vyasa."

Rep.: "Though the Maharishi is proficient in the Hindu texts mentioned by you, T.M. is something that he discovered all by himself. Since T.M is his discovery, the Maharishi has a patent on it."

Ashok: "Are you saying that T.M. is a trademark, like Coca Cola or Pepsi?"

Rep.: "Yes, you are catching my drift."

Ashok: "Let me put it differently. In my course, I will be discussing the theory behind the technique of T.M. just like the way I discuss the theories of Yoga and Zen meditation. As a professor of philosophy, I will be discussing the ideas of the Maharishi's T.M., the way I discuss the Freudian theory of psychoanalysis. Are you saying that if I use the word psychoanalysis in the title of my course, I could be sued by Anna Freud?"

Rep.: "That is different. Freud did not register his name or his method the way the Maharishi registered his method of T.M."

Ashok: "Is not the method of T.M. already discussed in the Yoga system?"

Rep.: "Yes!"

Ashok: "Did not the Maharishi get the method from the Yoga system?"

Rep.: "Yes and no. The Maharishi might have got it from his readings of the Yoga and other systems of Hindu philosophy. But T.M. is his brand that he discovered before anyone else did."

Ashok: "I have studied the *Yogasutras* and have translated the text, which I use in my course. I have taught yoga for five years. I have read the Maharishi's works carefully. Don't you think that qualifies me to teach the theory behind the method of T.M.?"

Rep.: "Sorry, you are still not trained by the Maharishi."

Ashok: "How long is the training before you could teach T.M. to others?"

Rep.: "It takes six weeks to learn the theory and practice of T.M. from the Maharishi."

Ashok: "Have you had your six weeks training?"

Rep.: "Yes."

Ashok: "Are you a trained master of T.M.?"

Rep.: "Yes."

Ashok: "What are your other academic qualifications?"

Rep.: "I have a B.A. degree in business."

Ashok: "Do you think that you can teach T.M. without any training in the Hindu philosophy and religion?"

Rep.: "The Maharishi gave some lectures on Hindu culture and religion during the course of six weeks."

Ashok: "If I understand you correctly, what you are saying is that the six weeks of training by the Maharishi makes you an expert to teach T.M., which you know is an offshoot of the Yoga method."

Rep.: "Yes."

Ashok: "Let me indulge you a bit by giving you an example. Suppose a student from India who had just obtained a B.A. degree comes to the United States to take a course on nuclear physics from a famous professor. After completing the course, he goes back to India to tell everyone including the Ph.D.'s in physics that he is more qualified to teach nuclear physics than they. How will you react to it if you were one of those Ph.D.'s in nuclear physics?"

Rep.: "That is different."

Ashok: "How so?"

Rep.: "Because T.M. has been discovered by the Maharishi and it can be taught only by him or by people trained by him."

Ashok: "Is not T.M. a body of knowledge, which can be taught by anyone or by the Maharishi or people trained by the Maharishi?"

Rep.: "Yes and no. T.M. is a body of knowledge but it can't be taught by anyone except the Maharishi or people trained by him."

Ashok: "Though I did not get my training with the Maharishi, yet I have a Ph.D. in philosophy, I have studied the Yoga system, and I have taught yoga for five years. Does not that qualify me to discuss the ideas behind the T.M. system?:

Rep.:   (getting impatient with my questions) "I have told you repeatedly that you cannot. It is against the law."

Ashok: "I still think that I have the qualifications to teach Yoga, Zen, and T.M."

Rep.:   "I want to warn you not to use the word T.M. in the title of your course. If you do so, you have been made aware of the consequences."

At this juncture, the T.M. representative got up and left.

Since a copy of the letter was also received by the President of our college, he called me to settle the issue before the course commenced during the next week. After my conversation with the T.M. representative, I went to see the President and summarized the highlights of my encounter. The President was disappointed and asked me to rectify the situation so that the college was not involved in any law suit. I told the President that I had decided to teach the same material as planned but the title would be changed to "Creative Living Though Yoga, Zen, and M.M." The President asked me what the letters M.M. stood for? I replied, "Malhotra Meditation."

The President was pleased that I changed T.M. to M.M., but was displeased with the T.M. organization for curbing our freedom of teaching. He decided to pay the T.M. in the same coin by forbidding the local T.M. group from using the campus facilities free of charge.

Ashok Kumar Malhotra

Bhagwan Rajneesh
and
Dynamic Meditation

Bhagwan Rajneesh was unlike the other gurus. While others talked about god and spirituality, he openly talked about sex. He regarded all the past religions as anti-laughter and anti-life. They were too restrictive and could not accept a human being in its totality. Not a single religion of the past emphasized laughter or fun. Rajneesh called himself a rebel of the highest order because he was born to break all rules. His disciples were rich Indian and Western intellectuals who were disenchanted with the negativity of existentialism.

Though I never met Rajneesh in person, I was first introduced to his ideas and personality through a professor of his at the University of Hawaii. I was taking a course on Yoga from Professor Saksena who was also Rajneesh's teacher at Sagar University in India. Professor Saksena was a well-known scholar of philosophy who was hired by the University of Hawaii because of his reputation. Professor Saksena was the very reason that I had come to the University of Hawaii to study philosophy. As I went to the first Yoga class, Saksena came in on time. He brought no books or class notes with him. As he walked into the classroom, he looked at me and asked me: "Why are you taking this course?" I told him that I was interested in Patanjali's *Yogasutras* and had heard from the students that he was a terrific teacher. Saksena said: "You should not be in the class because every Indian knows something about the Yoga system. It will be a waste of time to spend fifteen weeks to learn about what you already know." I pleaded that I

Instant Nirvana

wanted to listen to his interpretation of the *Yogasutras*, which would be valuable to me. Saksena let me sit in the class the first day and asked me not to come anymore. Though I was unhappy with this treatment, I felt privileged that I could attend the class for one day.

Saksena started his lecture by telling the story of his teaching years in India, where he met this very strange student whose name was Rajneesh. Saksena had the habit of telling his students on the first day of his classes that the main goal of philosophy was not to answer questions but to question all answers. He required of his students to raise at least one question during each of his lectures. In one of his classes, all of his students except one, raised questions. The student who did not ask any question was Rajneesh. Professor Saksena was perturbed by the Rajneesh's open disregard. During the second meeting of the class, everyone except Rajneesh asked questions. Saksena looked at Rajneesh and asked him in a stern voice: "Rajneesh, have you listened to my rule regarding raising at least one question in each class." Rajneesh replied: "Yes, I heard you Professor Saksena." Saksena: "If you have heard me, why are not you raising questions like every one else? Why are you disobeying your instructor?" Rajneesh did not answer. This silence infuriated Professor Saksena who asked again: "Why are you silent? Are you pretending to be dumb? You must have some questions. Please tell me why aren't you raising any?" Rajneesh, who was having a hell of a good time by riling Saksena up, said: "I have no questions to ask." Saksena, who was losing his patience, retorted: "Why don't you have any questions?" Rajneesh replied with a smile on his face: "Dr. Saksena, the reason that I don't have any questions is because I have all the answers."

At this juncture, Saksena lost his cool and told Rajneesh to get out and to never come back to his class. Rajneesh who had the upper hand in this entire episode got up and left the class. A few days later, Rajneesh had dropped out of the University and had left for the Himalayas to practice meditation. After spending a few years there, Rajneesh returned and declared himself Bhagwan, which meant the "blessed one;" "one who had found himself or one who had returned home." From then on, Rajneesh started ordaining disciples into his special brand of spiritual practice called Dynamic Meditation.

Three Encounters with the Dalai Lama: Encounter at Syracuse University

During the late 1970's, Dr. Houston Smith of Syracuse University had organized a historic panel on compassion and had invited the Dalai Lama to be the keynote speaker. He had asked me to be one of the commentators. I was very excited to get such an invitation and felt very fortunate that I would come face-to-face with the real Dalai Lama.

After accepting the invitation, I talked to the president of our College to give him the good news. As a wonderful and supporting person, the president gave me the go-ahead for participating in such a momentous event.

Since I couldn't contain myself with exuberance, I decided to share this news with other members of the college community. One of these was Fred Ermlich. He was our college's Ombudsman, who was a former priest. When I told him that I was going to comment on the

Instant Nirvana

Dalai Lama's speech at the Syracuse University, he was very excited for me. However, he asked me whether he could accompany me to hear the Dalai Lama. Since I could invite a guest, I told him that it would be a wonderful opportunity for him to join me.

I was curious as to why Fred was so excited to meet with the Dalai Lama. He told me that it was his dream to meet the Dalai Lama because "meeting him would be like having an audience with the Pope."

On the assigned day, Fred and I got into my car and we started driving from Oneonta to Syracuse. During this short journey of two hours, Fred and I had a long discussion about why he had dropped out of the priesthood. He told me that he got into the priesthood because his mother wanted one of her children to be in the religious business. Just to make his mother happy, he joined the priesthood. As the time passed, he came to the realization that he was not made for priesthood because he liked women too much. There was a real desire in him to get married and to have children. This desire could not be satisfied if he remained as a priest. So one day, he took enough courage to approach the topic with his mother. He explained to her his reasons for dropping out of priesthood. Though his mother was unhappy with his decision, she was very understanding and supportive. She gave him the blessings so that he could drop out without any guilt. However, she asked him to promise to be compassionate towards other by serving humanity.

It took us close to two hours to reach Syracuse. As we arrived at the University, there was a lot of commotion. A number of buses had brought more than a few dozen Buddhist monks. As they walked out of the buses, their demeanor reflected reverence and peacefulness.

Ashok Kumar Malhotra

The monks were delighted that they would see and be seen with the Dalai Lama. Since the Dalai Lama was the embodiment of enlightenment, to be in the presence of such a great man was a wonderful dream that had come true for these monks. Fred was in a similar situation too because he was undergoing the same kind of excitement. He could feel the empathetic-sympathy by identifying himself with the exhilaration of the monks. Feeling this unusual thrill, Fred exclaimed that this was going to be the greatest treat for which he had been waiting for all his life.

As we walked through the campus to reach the Lecture Hall where the Dalai Lama was to speak, there was a great deal of awe-inspiring commotion. We could see the entire Hall packed with students, faculty, administrators, and members of the community as well as both the Buddhist and Hindu monks. The excitement of the audience was so contagious that one could sense it through every pore of one's body.

When we entered the Hall, we saw Dr. Houston Smith standing next to the stage talking in a gentle voice to his students and colleagues. From which I could surmise that his students respected him a lot.

There was a great deal of sound and fury in the Hall. All of a sudden, the sound died out and the people stopped talking. Dr. Houston Smith announced that he was glad to inform the audience that it was a great day for the people of America, New York and especially Syracuse that his Holiness the Dalai Lama was giving this speech on compassion at the Syracuse University. He was grateful that along with the Dalai Lama, a number of scholars from other parts of the State had arrived there to participate in this rare encounter with one of the greatest of living human beings. Moreover, it was his extraordinary privilege to introduce one of the most lovable and compassionate persons on this earth, the Dalai Lama of Tibet.

The Dalai Lama, who was dressed up in a reddish-ochre robe entered from the back door and came all the way to the stage. Dr Houston Smith folded both his hands put them in front of his chest and said "Namaste," which meant: "From the core of my heart I greet you."

The Dalai Lama spoke on compassion choosing his words very carefully. He declared his full allegiance to non-violence as a personal and political tool. In his speech to his Western audience, the Dalai Lama tried to convey that there was an inner universe that was as rich as or richer than the outer world. He was there to introduce the Western audience to this exciting inner universe. The great mystery of this inner journey could be conducted by anyone who openly and honestly expressed his love and compassion for others by helping them, feeding them, and educating them.

I listened to the Dalai Lama intently and was much impressed by his genuine compassion and concern for the welfare of humanity. But my own rebellious spirit wanted to counter his arguments. I had felt that the people of Tibet had not harmed anyone for centuries. They were the most peaceful and compassionate people on this earth, who were the model of compassion. But, why this wonderful expression of compassion did them in? Why did the Chinese take over Tibet so easily? Why did they make the Dalai Lama a spiritual-king without a country? All this made no sense! Though it was wonderful of the Dalai Lama to espouse the doctrine of compassion for all including the Chinese, it made no sense that the people of Tibet, who listened to the Dalai Lama's interpretation of the message of the Buddha, should be put in such a precarious situation that they were either without a country or were subjugated as slave by the communist regime of China.

I was bubbling with rebellion and a genuine compassion for the misfortune that had struck the peace loving people of Tibet. When my turn came to comment on the Dalai Lama's speech, I vented my feelings of dissatisfaction with this unfortunate state of affairs. I conveyed in clear terms, which were similar to Gandhi, who had used his philosophy of non-violence against the British rule in India. When an American reporter asked Gandhi whether the same non-violent tactics would have worked with Hitler, Gandhi's response was in the negative. My reaction to the Dalai Lama's speech was similar to Gandhi. I told the Dalai Lama that the people of Tibet would never get their land back from the Chinese unless some great power like the USA or USSR helped with arms to oust the Chinese. After listening to my comments, the Dalai Lama walked over to me. He put his hand on my shoulder and addressed me: "You are from India, our neighbor: The land of Gandhi–the model of non-violence; the land that gave us the compassionate-one, the Buddha. How could you ignore their example and talk about violence to save the people of Tibet? I am against all violence. I do not believe in the maxim: "an eye for an eye;" but in a different maxim which is "to turn the other cheek that has not been hit yet." I told the compassionate one that this seemed good in theory but the people of Tibet would be paying a dear price with their life, liberty and happiness, which they would not be able to achieve because of his policy of non-violent compassion. I appealed to him to think about this decision very carefully and to visualize the long-term effects. The Dalai Lama reacted by pointing out that he would be proven right in the long run. Compassion would be victorious and that was his firm belief!

I stopped arguing with him at that point because I knew that he was thoroughly convinced with his decision, which I or any one else could not change.

My friend Fred, who was sitting next me, was in a blissful state because he had never seen or encountered a religious leader of that stature as close as he was encountering the Dalai Lama at this moment. Next to him a number of Buddhist monks had prostrated themselves on the ground to show their reverence for their Buddha on this earth. Since my further arguing would have taken away from this wonderful ambiance, I stopped and let the discussion cease at that moment.

Encounter in New York City

Ever since my first encounter with the Dalai Lama, I had been thinking about him and had been talking to the President of our College about inviting the Dalai Lama to Oneonta. During August 2003, an opportunity arose because the Dalai Lama was visiting New York City. One day the President called and told me that I should go to New York to attend a special session, which the Dalai Lama was presenting in one of the theaters in the Times Square area.

I was very excited about the fact that I would have a second opportunity to go and see the Dalai Lama in person. Since my son Ravi lived in New York City, I called him to ask him a favor so that he could buy a ticket for me to attend the Dalai Lama's lecture. Ravi was happy to do so.

On the assigned day and I picked up my ticket. I had brought my camera with me to take pictures of the Dalai Lama. I parked my car at the nearby parking area. In front of the theater there were many people from different parts of the country and the world. There was a long line around the entire block where people had been standing for hours to get into the theater.

I followed the line and got a place far in the back. As I stood there, I started a conversation with a few people who were next to me. One couple that was in its 30's had been following the Dalai Lama all around the world. They told me that they would have given anything to be in the presence of the Dalai Lama that day.

I told the couple that I had encountered the Dalai Lama a number of years ago. This day I had come to deliver a letter from the President of our College so that the Dalai Lama could visit our campus. I asked the couple whether they found the Dalai Lama to be a good speaker. The couple was unanimous in its praise. They felt that the Dalai Lama was a compassionate human being and a fabulous speaker. Our students as well as faculty would be very lucky to have him as one of our keynote speakers in the future.

While we were having this discussion, the line moved slowly. It must have taken us close to an hour to finally make it to the entrance hall. There were a number of security guards at the doors who checked all our possessions. When they saw my camera, they asked me to leave it at the desk because no pictures were allowed.

Instant Nirvana

As I was carrying a letter from the President of the College, I walked all the way to the front so that I could get a seat across from this stage. I was very fortunate that I did find a vacant seat somewhere in the middle section across from the stage. As I sat down, I saw a couple from Tibet. I introduced myself and found out that they were acquainted with the Dalai Lama. I asked them as to how I could meet with the Dalai Lama so that I could deliver an invitation to him to visit our campus. The couple told me that it would be difficult to communicate directly with the Dalai Lama because of security concerns. However, I could meet with his assistant and give him the letter of invitation.

As we were chit chatting, the entire theater came to a total silence. A handsome man came to the microphone and announced that he was Richard Gere and was fortunate to be the one to introduce his holiness the Dalai Lama. Before he could introduce the main speaker, he would be interested in doing some house cleaning that included no picture taking, no noise, total silence etc. Moreover, he told the audience that the Dalai Lama would be taking close to 15 minutes to arrive at the stage. If during this time anybody had any questions, they should come to the stage to inquire.

This was a golden opportunity for me. I walked over to the stage and introduced myself to Richard Gere. I told him that my name was Dr. Ashok Malhotra and I was a professor of philosophy at the SUNY College at Oneonta. I had brought a letter of invitation for the Dalai Lama so that he could be invited as a keynote speaker to address the student body at SUNY College. Richard Gere extended his arm and shook my hand. He told me that he was the master of ceremony for that day and had no authority to arrange the Dalai Lama's speeches. Though he could not arrange, yet someone in the Tibet House in New York, could help me out. I handed the letter of invitation, thanked him and came back to my seat.

To my surprise, the person sitting next to me was no other than the actress Goldie Hawn. We exchanged glances and she gave her usual baby-like smile. I introduced myself to her and she did the same. She told me that she was a follower of the great Dalai Lama and would not miss his speech and presence for anything. I congratulated her for her deep devotion.

As the Dalai Lama appeared on the stage, it produced a meditative silence in the theater. The Dalai Lama sat down and started reading his speech, which was translated into English by one of his translators. He talked about compassion as the answer to world's problems. He described the eight-fold path consisting of *Shila* (moral training), *Dhyana* (meditation) and *Prajna* (wisdom) and recited verses from *The Thirty Seven Practices of Bodhisattva*. In his discourse, the message was the same that he had delivered a number of years ago. He reiterated the principles of non-violence and compassion. We were not born to just make money but to take care of others through service. The place was packed with devotees, who had come from all over the world to unstress themselves and be in the glow of the master.

Instant Nirvana

Dalai Lama's Philosophy in a Nutshell

In his book on *"How to Expand Love,"* the Dalai Lama presents the meaning of life in a nutshell. He asserts that "we are not here to just acquire wealth but to do something meaningful that is directed towards the welfare of humanity as a whole." Our responsibility extends to all humanity.

In order to fit it into his philosophical/humanistic perspective, religion for the Dalai Lama means "being motivated by compassion and love, while respecting the rights of others."

The quintessence of religion is to serve others rather than to dominate them.

At the core of the Dalai Lama's philosophy is compassionate humanism where the emphasis is put on one's kind nature through which one compassionately serves others continuously.

The real nature of the human mind is to be pure and empty. It is compared to the blue sky where the clouds can temporarily envelop it but pass without leaving any trace behind.

Likewise, various emotions of fear, aggressiveness, anger, jealousy and hatred might overwhelm the mind by agitating it, but like the clouds, these emotions do not touch the purity of the mind. The nature of the mind is clear light. Defilements are superficial.

As we contemplate the real and authentic nature of the mind, we will discover it to be that of compassion. Compassion means "an intense desire to serve others in order to alleviate their suffering."

Ashok Kumar Malhotra

There is a practical down-to-earth method to cultivate compassion towards others through nurturing equality through the following:

1. Say Good Bye to Enmity

Visualize or contemplate a friend, an enemy and a neutral person. Ask yourself the questions: "What does attract me towards this person?" "What does repel me about this individual?" and "What does keep me neutral of feelings and emotions towards this human being?" Now envision each one of them to be a human being, who seeks happiness and avoids pain. Accept each one as equal in its seeking of happiness and avoidance of pain. Place this feeling of equality in your mind and nurture it continuously till it becomes part of your mindset and the entire being.

2. Visualize Change

Visualize or contemplate friends, enemies and neutral people to change constantly never staying in any one of these states for any length of time. Imagine each one to be transforming and becoming its opposite. The one to whom you love becomes the one you hate; the one to whom you hate becomes the one towards whom you are neutral and the one towards whom you are neutral becomes the one to whom you love. "Decide not to single out any one for one kind of treatment."

There are seven steps of inculcating compassionate humanism!

1. Create positive inclination towards others!

2. Remember the kindness that has been showered on you by members of the family and friends!

3. Inculcate kindness towards others!

4. Acknowledge others' suffering! Take sympathetic-empathetic attitude towards other's pain by learning to love them.

5. Cultivate the desire to alleviate other's suffering. Develop compassion! Release others of suffering by enhancing their happiness.

6. Make a total commitment towards altruism.

7. Make love and compassion towards others as a way of life.

Encounter in Cape Town, South Africa

During December 1999, I had been invited to attend the prestigious Parliament of World Religions. It was being held from December 1-8, in Cape Town, South Africa. There were more than 6000 people of various religious persuasions, who had assembled to partake in the spiritual gifts of humankind as presented in their religious books and practice. Besides reading and discussing papers on topics relating to the diverse religious traditions of humankind, the highlight of the Parliament was a meeting with and listening to such speakers as Nelson Mandela and the Dalai Lama. Moreover, since the old millennium was coming to an end and a new one was to begin in less than 23 days, the Parliament had offered a challenge to the presenters to submit their compassionate projects that were going to make the world a better place during the next century. These projects were to be judged by a jury that would decide which of these would become "a model of service to humanity." Out of a few thousand of such projects, one hundred most outstanding were to be picked and be declared as models for others to imbibe. Since through the "SUNY Learn and Serve in India" study abroad program, I had helped start an Indo-International School for the 50 underprivileged children of Dundlod, India, I had presented a panel on the project to the members of the Parliament. During the panel, I had highlighted the fact that this was the first of many schools that we were going to build in India to deal with the illiteracy problem that was plaguing the poorest of poor children of India. Since our goal was to promote literacy among the children and adults throughout the world, we were raising funds to construct a new building for the Indo-International School in Dundlod during the new millennium. The SUNY Oneonta student and faculty volunteers, who would also raise the needed funds for the project, would construct the new school building. This first school would be one among many that would be opened in India and rest of the world to deal with the problem of illiteracy among the underprivileged female and other minority children.

Since the Indo-International School in Dundlod had already proved to be a model for improving the disparity in poverty-stricken areas like Dundlod, Rajasthan, Rabbi Avraham Soetendorp of the Netherlands, who was the founder of the Dutch Hoop voor Kinder (Hope for Children) Foundation, recognized our project to be a model that could be used by his and other similar organizations to develop schools for the underprivileged children of humanity. On December 8, 1999, Rabbi Soetendorp along with other members of the jury selected our Indo-International School venture to be one of the projects that excelled in its approach to solving one of the most oppressing problems of humanity, which was that of illiteracy. Of course, I was delighted that our project was chosen. To embellish this joy, I was asked to present to his Holiness the Dalai Lama, the Indo-International School project as "a model of a gift of service to humanity" for the new Millennium. I stood up among the 100 winners of the outstanding compassionate projects and gave a five-minute long speech while presenting my gift of service to humanity. The Dalai Lama acknowledged its acceptance. This was my third encounter with the Dalai Lama and this time I got his blessings to continue doing the compassionate work by spreading literacy throughout India and the world by opening Indo-International Schools for the underprivileged children of humanity.

The Saga of Sai Baba

I had received blessings of the Dalai Lama at the Parliament of World Religions at Cape Town, South Africa. With this very uplifting spiritual sanction from the members of the Parliament of Religions and the Dalai Lama, I was firmly convinced that we were going to be successful in our endeavor to establish the new school.

This overflow of optimism materialized into starting the new Millennium by building and inaugurating our first Indo-International School for 150 underprivileged children in Dundlod, a remote village of Rajasthan, India. The school was a landmark accomplishment of the Ninash Foundation, a charitable organization, established by me "to promote literacy among children and adults throughout the world." To accomplish this great feat, we had received assistance in the USA, from the student and faculty volunteers of SUNY College at

Ashok Kumar Malhotra

Oneonta and in India, from Dr. Ganga Singh, who had been volunteering her time to supervise the running of the Indo-International School in Dundlod.

Ganga was a firm devotee of the Sai Baba for more than a dozen years and was totally taken in by his spiritual and miraculous powers. Whenever she needed any kind of help whether it was financial, psychological, social or spiritual, she would take a special pilgrimage to Puttaparthi, the abode of the Sai Baba where she spent a week to do "seva" or "selfless service." Ganga would live in a room, sleep on the floor, clean and help in kitchen of the Sai Baba's Ashram. In return, she would have the privileged *"darshan"* or the opportunity to see the Sai Baba in person. Because she was a regular visitor to the Ashram, Ganga was given the opportunity to sit in the front row during the *darshan* time. Moreover, she was also provided the prospect to write down her wish list on a piece of paper, which the Sai Baba might pick up from her hands. On her wish list, Ganga usually put down matters relating to the financial help she needed to build schools for the poor children of India and many times, after each visit to the Ashram, her wishes were miraculously fulfilled. All this embellished her faith in the divine incarnation of the Sai Baba. She believed wholeheartedly that the Sai Baba was a walking/talking living god on earth.

Since we had just completed and inaugurated the first Indo-International School in Dundlod, Ganga had asked me to accompany her to see the Sai Baba for a few days. I had observed Ganga's complete dedication to the Indo-International School and was so impressed with her generous volunteering of time that I accepted her invitation.

Instant Nirvana

Both of us flew from Delhi to Bangalore where my brother and his wife joined us on this holy pilgrimage. We rented a private car to go from Bangalore to Puttaparthi. The three-hour long journey was pleasant. When we arrived in Puttaparthi, the entire town and all its shops seemed to be devoted to Sai Baba. Every shop was selling something relating to Sai Baba whether they were books, clothes, jewelry, food or souvenirs. The pictures of Sai Baba were liberally displayed everywhere and when anyone greeted us; they addressed us with the phrase "Jai Sai." The entire town and its people were preoccupied with Sai Baba and his glory because the town's economy was totally dependent on the magnetic pull of Sai Baba, who on a daily basis, brought a throng of visitors from all over the globe.

Since Ganga had been a frequent visitor, she already had a room assigned to her whereas my brother, his wife and I had to stand in line to get accommodations for a few nights. Since I was a foreign passport holder, they rented the room to us for a moderate price. However, the room that had three cots was without any sheets, blankets or pillows. When we asked for these items, we were told to go to the Sai Baba Commissary run by the Sai Trust where we could purchase these items for a cheap price. Though there was a huge line of people waiting to buy these items for a few nights' stay at the Ashram, the prices turned out to be reasonable. While we waited in line, we noticed that everyone who was there had a deeply rooted faith in the *avatar* hood of the Sai Baba. They greeted each other with "Jai Sai" and showed in their eyes, walk and demeanor that they were dedicated to the Sai Baba and his mission.

Ashok Kumar Malhotra

The room had cots woven with jute rope that were uncomfortable pieces of equipment to be used for eight hours each night for three days. I was accustomed to sleeping on very comfortable beds because of my chronic backache. Any bed that did not meet those standards was a real pain in my back. Since I had promised Ganga that I would come with her to see Sai Baba, I was going to stick to my commitment even though I was going to spend three miserable nights on that uncomfortable cot.

Ganga had told us that if we would like to have the Baba's *darshan* in morning, we had to get up very early to be standing in the line by 4 AM at the latest because others would be there even before that. Since the bed was utterly uncomfortable, I could not get a wink of sleep. I was restless till 4 AM and then walked out of the bedroom quietly to stand in line for the Baba's *darshan*. My brother and his wife were fast asleep on those uncomfortable cots and were not interested in having Baba's *darshan* at that hour.

There must have been more than 500 people already waiting since midnight. Looking at their faith, dedication and patience, I told myself not to be skeptical and to go with the flow. Be here and now and get the most spiritual benefit from this morning outing at the spiritual Ashram of the Sai Baba! I convinced myself that something special was waiting for me because otherwise I would not have been so foolish to be treating myself to such an uncomfortable bed, a sleepless night and a morning where I was surrounded by more than 500 dedicated souls. I heard people talk about Sai Baba as if he "were all knowing," who had already decided for each one of us the purpose of our visit to that place.

Instant Nirvana

Through his all-knowing-consciousness, the Baba had already picked the most dedicated ones to be sitting in the front seat so that he would pick their wish list.

After listening to their enthusiastic and pious talk, I told myself to have more faith and cleanse my mind of all doubt. I should put myself in Baba's mind and his hands. I told myself that since he had brought me there through the agency of Ganga, there was a mysterious purpose to be fulfilled through all this discomfort I was undergoing. Otherwise, who, in his right state of mind, after building a school for the underprivileged children during the start of the new Millennium, would be treating himself so shoddily by sleeping on a rock-hard bed, and standing in the middle of the night in a foreign street among 500 strangers from all over the globe to see this diminutive who had girlish feet and hair-set that looked like a bee-hive? What on earth was I doing there? The moment that thought came through my mind, I pushed it out to indicate my faith and determination to stick with it and fulfill my commitment to Ganga.

As I was occupied with my turbulent mind and its gymnastics, a sweet looking man belonging to the Sai brigade came close to where I was standing and asked the man in front of me to come forward because he was chosen to be the one sitting at the front of that line. The man was so delighted about his fate that he had tears of joy coming down from his eyes. He screamed with pleasure "Jai Sai," "You are the real Avatar," and "You are God." While saying those words of exultation, the man obediently moved to the front as he followed the guard. Though every time a guard came close by, I gave him a nervous smile so that he would notice and take pity on me by choosing me but it was of no avail.

Ashok Kumar Malhotra

I spent the next few hours in the line that moved at a snails' pace. By six or so we were all asked to be seated and stay quiet. Anyone who made any noise was told to stop that behavior. Almost everyone had brought a wish list with the hope that Sai would turn his compassionate eye on him or her and pick that list from their hands. It was the greatest privilege to be chosen to sit in front of the line and then the second best gift was when the Baba picked the wish list from the devotee's hands. If your thoughts were noble and you possessed good karmas, you would be the first one in the line and your wish list would be selected. From all over the globe devotees had come with the hope of being in that privileged situation where they sat closest to Sai Baba to experience the most intimate glow of the God on earth. Almost everyone sitting around me looked like an embodiment of spiritual reverence and was anticipating the *darshan* of the Sai Baba, the *avatar*, the human form of God on the earth.

Everyone including me was sitting reverently on the cold marble floor. Most of the devotees were either meditating or praying or lost in their thoughts while their eyes were closed. However, I kept my eyes open in order to be the first to get a glimpse of Sai Baba.

As this spiritual spectacle was unfolding in front of my eyes, all of a sudden this long awaited encounter happened. A diminutive man with black curly hair wearing a red robe appeared in front of the audience. His right hand was up to greet and bless the devotees. While he walked his robe trailed behind on the marble, a reminder of a woman's wedding dress. The long robe gave the Baba a tall and slender look. He looked frail as he moved his head towards the audience. Devotees, who were sitting in the front row, were clutching their wish list in between both hands. They were looking at the Baba with hungry eyes hoping that he would look at them and would pick their letters.

Baba walked very slowly as if he was gliding on the marble floor. He paid special attention to the familiar faces occupying the front row and picked a few of these letters thus making these people as the chosen ones whose mission was successfully completed. Those who were selected were elated and thanked their lucky stars whereas the rest of us remained sitting while clutching our wish lists. As I was sitting in the sixth or seventh row with a list of my own, seeing the Baba right across from my row, I lifted up my list and made a sound saying "Baba please pick this one," a couple of other devotees subdued me by telling me to hush up. They physically stopped me from raising my hands up in the air. After crossing the length of the hall, the Baba's *darshan* was over and he left the temple for his living/business quarters.

The entire *darshan* was so short that I started wondering about the amount of time, money spent, and discomfort endured by hundreds of these devotees. What was the meaning of all this? Was it a worthwhile experience or a big waste of resources? As I glanced at the hall full of devotees, I was wondering what was going through their minds now that the *darshan* was over? I had taken two and one half hours flight from Delhi to Bangalore and a three-hour long car journey from Bangalore to Puttaparthi along with a sleepless four hours in hard bed and almost three hours of waiting in line and sitting on the cold marble floor. I did all this for a few minutes of having a glimpse of the Baba and before I could make sense of it, it was all over. Instead of feeling happy or elated or content, I felt disappointed and foolish.

As I left the marble floor, I took a walk outside the main door of the Ashram to look at the Town's people, who were going through their usual daily chores. My mind kept on asking whether all this was worth the time, money and effort. My answer was that those who were chosen to sit in the front row to get the closest look at the divine incarnation and those whose letters were picked up by the Baba were blissed out for their luck whereas rest of us came out with a sense of disappointment.

Sai Baba's Practical Wisdom

Since before coming to the Puttaparthi Ashram, I had read various books, articles and pamphlets on Sai Baba's Philosophy, I was more impressed with the written word than the actual personal encounter.

Sai Baba's philosophy is a simplified version of the *Advaita Vedanta*. The goal of life is *Atman-Vidya* i.e. the knowledge of the eternal self. This is the common pursuit of all religions. This *Atman-Vidya* is possible through love and service towards humanity. Irrespective of their other beliefs, all religions are equal in emphasizing the importance of love and service, which are the surest paths towards enlightenment. Though Sai Baba emphasizes the daily practice of meditation and yet gives priority to love and service as the quickest ways towards *Atman* knowledge. In a mocking fashion, Sai Baba says: "An act of service is more valuable than one month spent on meditation."

Instant Nirvana

His advice to his followers of other religions is that he is not here to convert non-Hindus into becoming Hindus but to help others to flourish in their own faiths. Whether they are Muslims, Christians, Jews, Buddhists, Jains, Sikhs, Taoists and followers of Shinto, Sai Baba's recommendation to them is to mix together his teaching with their faiths. There is only one God. We are here to love Him, His Creation and other human beings. Service of others is the surest way to accomplish this. Sai Baba regards himself as the avatar or the material manifestation of this one God. Since he is the living God on earth, he could be appropriated through such names as Krishna, Christ and Buddha. His own life is an exemplification of the ideal of each religion, which is to serve everybody, feed everyone and love all humanity. As the avatar, Sai Baba not only speaks the truth, he is the truth.

Bibliography

B.B. Anand, G.S. Chhina, and Baldev Singh, "Some Aspects of Electroencephalographic Studies in Yoga," *Altered States of Consciousness*, edited by Charles Tart. New York: Doubleday, 1972.

Sri Aurobindo, *The Life Divine*. Calcutta: Acharya Publishing House, 1947.

Mick Brown: *The Spiritual Tourist: A Personal Odyssey through the Outer Reaches of Belief.* London: Bloomsbury Publishing, 1998.

Christianity Today, September 28, 1973.

William de Bary, *Sources of Indian Tradition*. New York: Columbia University Press, 1958.

Robert Ellwood, *Religious and Spiritual Groups in Modern America*. Englewood Cliffs, NJ: Prentice Hall, 1973.

David Haddon, "New Plant Thrives on a Spiritual Desert," *Christianity Today* (December 21, 1973).

J. Stillson Judah, *Hare Krishna and the Counterculture*. New York: Wiley-Interscience, 1974.

Akira Kasamatsu and Tomio Hirai, "An Electroencephalographic Study on the *Zen* Meditation (*Zazen*)," *Altered States of Consciousness*, edited by Charles Tart. New York: Doubleday, 1972.

Ken Kelley, "East Indian Teenager Says He is God," *Vogue*, March 1974.

Dalai Lama: *My Land and My People*. New York: Warner Books, 1997.

Instant Nirvana

Life, February 9, 1968.

Life, November 10, 1967.

S. K. Maitra, *The Philosophy of Sri Aurobindo.* Benaras: Benaras Hindu University, 1945.

A.K. Malhotra, *On Hindu Philosophies of Experience: Cults, Mysticism and Meditations.* Oneonta, NY: Oneonta Philosophy Studies, 1993.

A.K. Malhotra, *Transcreation of the Bhagavad Gita.* Englewood Cliffs, NJ: Prentice Hall, 1998.

A.K. Malhotra, *Instant Nirvana.* Oneonta, NY: Oneonta Philosophy Studies, 1999.

A.K. Malhotra, *An Introduction to Yoga Philosophy.* Aldershot, UK: Ashgate, 2001

A.K. Malhotra, *Wisdom of the Tao Te Ching: The Code of A Spiritual Warrior.* Oneonta, NY: Oneonta Philosophy Studies, 2002.

A.K. Malhotra, "Yoga Therapeutics: Philosophical, Scientific, and Humanistic Perspectives." A paper in a volume on *East West Whiteheadian Dialogue.* Oxford: Oxford University Press, 2007.

Robert McDermott and V.S. Naravane, *The Spirit of Modern of Modern India.* New York: Thomas Y. Crowell Company, 1974.

R.R. Michaels, M.J. Huber, and D.S. McCann, "Evaluation of Transcendental Meditation as a Method of Reducing Stress," *Science,* Vol. 92 (June 1976).

V.S. Naravane, *Modern Indian Thought.* Missouri: South Asia Book, 1978.

Ashok Kumar Malhotra

Jacob Needleman, *The New Religions*. New York: Doubleday & Co., 1970.

New Republic, November 17, 1973.

New York Times Magazine, December 9, 1973.

Newsweek, March 23, 1970.

Newsweek, May 15, 1972.

Newsweek, November 19, 1973.

Robert Pagano, Richard Rose, and Stephen Warrenburg, "Sleep During Transcendental Meditation," *Science*, Vol. 19 (January 1976).

Harrison Pope, *The Road East: America's New Discovery of Eastern Wisdom*. Boston: Beacon Press, 1974.

M.N. Roy, *The Historical Role of Islam*. Calcutta: Renaissance Publishers, 1958.

D.W. Shrader and A.K. Malhotra, *Pathways to Philosophy: A Multidisciplinary Approach*. Englewood Cliffs, NJ: Prentice Hall, 1996.

Walter T. Stace, *The Teachings of the Mystics*. New York: Mentor Book, 1960.

R.N. Tagore, *Personality*. Madras: Macmillan and Co. Limited, 1997.

S. Tejasananda, *A Short Life of Ramakrishna*. Calcutta: Advaita Ashram, 1980.

Time, May 12, 1975.

Time, October 13, 1975.

Time, August 4, 2003.

Time, January 29, 2007

Instant Nirvana

Raymond Van Over, ed., *Eastern Mysticism Volume One: The Near East and India.* New York: Mentor Book, 1977.

Robert Wallace and Herbert Benson, "The Physiology of Meditation," *Scientific American,* Vol. 226, No. 2 (1972).

Amy Weintraub, *Yoga for Depression: A Compassionate Guide to Relieve Suffering through Yoga.* New York: Broadway Books, 2004.

Ashok Kumar Malhotra

Oneonta Philosophy Studies
HISTORICAL AND CULTURAL PERSPECTIVES

Oneonta Philosophy Studies is a scholarly series that promotes exchange concerning traditional and contemporary issues in philosophy. Because comparative study often fosters appreciation and tolerance as well as understanding, special consideration is given to manuscripts that illuminate relationships between diverse or seemingly discrete views. Historical and cultural studies are especially welcome.

Submission is open to all – without regard to institutional affiliation, political preference, religious belief, gender, or national origin. Manuscripts are subject to external review. Published material does not necessarily reflect the views of the Editorial Board, the Philosophy Department, or the State University of New York.

A series such as this depends on the vision, good will, and labor of many. Special appreciation is extended to the *Asian Studies Development Program* (ASDP), *Global Scholarly Publications* (GSP), *Institute of Global Cultural Studies* (IGCS), *Society for Ancient Greek Philosophy* (SAGP), *Society for the Study of Islamic Philosophy and Science* (SSIPS), and the State University of New York at Oneonta – especially Michael Merilan (Dean of Science and Social Science), F. Daniel Larkin (Provost and Vice President for Academic Affairs) and Alan B. Donovan (President).

DOUGLAS W. SHRADER
EDITOR IN CHIEF

Books

  🙿 **Virtue, Order, Mind:**
Ancient, Modern, and Post-Modern Perspectives
Peter Vincent Amato, editor

On Choosing a Teacher: Plato's *Protagoras* (MARIE I. GEORGE); Words of Love: Rhetoric and Eros in Plato's *Phaedrus* (DOUGLAS W. SHRADER); Tragic *Katharsis* (MARTHA HUSAIN); *Metaphysics* Z and H: Spurious V. Genuine Genera (WALTER E. WEHRLE); Aquinas, Aristotle, and the Convertibility of Being and Truth (JAMES T. H. MARTIN); Toxic Shame and the Lonerganian Concept of Conversion (DENNIS D. KLEIN); Jonas on the Crisis for Modern Man (OSCAR MOHL & ANGELO JUFFRAS); A Roadmap for Ethics in the Twenty-First Century (EDDY SOUFFRANT); Communicative Rationality, Communicative Ethics and the Political Space of the Public Sphere (EVANGELOS KOBOLAKIS); A Pragmatic Reading of Gadamer's Philosophical Hermeneutics (VINCENT MARK VACCARO); Reconceiving Power and the Social Through Baudrillard (MARC HANES); A Feminist Analysis of Value-Neutral Observation (MAUREEN LINKER); Modernity, Kolakowski and Myth (PETER VINCENT AMATO).

1994 – 203 pages – ISBN 1-883058-16-3

  🙿●**Essays in Islamic Philosophy,**
Theology, and Mysticism
Parviz Morewedge

Basic Dimensions of Islamic Theology; Basic Concepts of Neoplatonism; Greek Sources of Some Islamic Philosophies of Being and Existence; Substance and Process Theories of the Self in Islamic Mysticism; Mystical Icons in Rumi's Metaphysical Poetry: Light, the Mediator and the Way; Sufism, Neoplatonism and Zaehner's Theistic Theory of Mysticism.

1995 – 265 + xxviii pages – ISBN 0-9633277-7-1

Ashok Kumar Malhotra

❧ Jean Paul Sartre's Existentialism in Literature and Philosophy
Ashok Kumar Malhotra

This book offers innovative approaches to the reading of the novel *Nausea*, considering it as a philosophical and a psychological novel, and as a work of art. After depicting the existential themes in *Nausea*, the author compares the existential philosophy of *Nausea* to that of *Being and Nothingness*, and then deals with the ethical and social dimensions of Sartre's philosophy before exploring the interconnection between philosophy, art, and literature.

1995 – 154 + x pages – ISBN 1-883058-14-7

❧ Seeds of Wisdom
Douglas W. Shrader, editor

Biological Research and Feminist Obligation (JENNIFER BURKE); Subjective versus Objective Reality: An Examination Through Physics and Philosophy (MICHAEL JOSEPH); Exploring the Universe: From Plato to Einstein and Beyond (ALEX SLATER); Observing, Observability, and the Importance of a Smiler: A Partial Defense of Strawsonian Events (DAVID MIGUEL GRAY); Follow Your Bliss: The Philosophy of Joseph Campbell (ANGELA CASE); Concepts of Self: East and West (GABRIELLE LEVIN); Quality, Love, and Madness: Pirsig versus Plato (KERRI NICHOLAS); Nietzsche's Appropriative Representation *or* Is the Overman a Hermaphrodite? (JOHN DEVINE); The Impossibilities, Irrationality, and Contradictions of Immanuel Kant's Ethical Theories (DAVID SCHAAF); Descartes and Nietzsche (TATIANA ZELIKINA)

1997 – 167 + xii pages – ISBN 1-883058-08-2

❧ Language, Ethics, and Ontology
Douglas W. Shrader, editor

Between Eastern and Western Thought: Individuation in a Western Setting (JOHN R. HARTMANN); The Paradigm of

Instant Nirvana

Emptiness: A Commentary on the *Diamond Sutra* (DANIEL J. BRISTOL); Rational Systematic Thought: Aristotle and Ancient Cultures (JOHN F. VELONA); Evolution of the One During the Early Medieval Period: Plotinus to Proclus (DAVID SCHAAF); Inversion of Fate: Boethius' Philosophy From Within (DAVID JUSTIN HODGE); The Nature of Rhetoric in Plato's *Gorgias* (ANNA CHRISTINA S. RIBEIRO); Discussing an Education, as Found in the *Phaedrus* (KEVIN GOETZ); Existence Communication and the Arbitrary Nature of Language (JEFFREY F. DUECK); On the Priority of Epistemic Issues to the Metaphysical Issues of Realism (DARIN SOMMA); Surface Spectral Reflectance and Color Objectivism (CHRISTOPHER O'CALLAGHAN); Events, Objects, Tropes, and Explanation (DAVID MIGUEL GRAY); Nietzsche and the Eternal Recurrence (DAVID MORGAN SVOLBA); The Possibility of Permissible Suicide Within Kant's Ethical Theory (PAUL NGUYEN); Emotions, Gender, and Kantian Morality (EMILY D. PORTER); Woman Philosopher: An Oxymoron? (HAZEL E. BARNES)

1998 – 352 + xvi pages – ISBN 1-883058-74-0

ಐ Children of Athena
Douglas W. Shrader, editor

Temporal Incongruity in Zeno of Elea and its Philosophical Consequences (JEFFERY M.J. MURPHY); Does the Ontological Argument Need Salvaging? (ERIN KATHLEEN CARTER); Putnam, Realism and PERCEPTION (CLINTON TOLLEY); Great Perfection: The Practical Phenomenology of Tibetan Buddhism (DANIEL J. BRISTOL); Counter-Intuitive Ethics (MEGHAN TADEL); The Thinker as Poet (ROBB E. EASON); Nietzsche's Use of Metaphor (JOHN HARTMANN); Wittgensteinian Hermeneutics? (KEVIN GOETZ); "Hear Say Yes in Joyce": Otherness, Gender, and Derridian Repetition (LITIA PERTA); A Critical Re-Evaluation of the Esoteric Character of Maimonides' Guide of the Perplexed (MICHAEL FRAZER); Apollonian, Dionysian and Socratic Views: A Nietzschian Exegesis (G. J. SCHWENK); Anti-Essentialism and Re-Identification (MICHAEL D. DAY); Contemporary Analytic Philosophy as Reflected in the Work of

Ashok Kumar Malhotra

Monty Python (GARY HARDCASTLE); When Artists Read Philosophers: From Modernism to Postmodernism (JERE PAUL SURBER)

1999 – 334 + xxii pages – ISBN 1-883058-67-8

ᛒ Instant Nirvana:
Americanization of Mysticism and Meditation
Ashok Kumar Malhotra

Mysticism in the Hindu Tradition; Instant Nirvana: Hindu Mysticism in the West; Meditation: Yoga, Zen, and T.M.; Encounters and Experiences with the Gurus.

First edition: 1999 – 128 + xvi pages – ISBN 1-883058-01-5

Second edition: 2007 – 160 + xviii pages

ᛒ **The Fractal Self**
Douglas W. Shrader, editor

Hegel And Shankaracharya: On the Non-Dualistic 'I' (PRIYADARSHI SHUKLA); The Nature of Mind in Tibetan Buddhist Ethical Theory (DANIEL J. BRISTOL); Buddha, Kant, and the Ethical Consequences of Suicide (KATHERINE COLLINS); Justice Outside the Polis in Aristotle's *Politics* and *Nicomachean Ethics* (TARA K. HOGAN); The Freedom That Fear Has Wrought (BRETT BISGROVE); An Analysis of Deontic Logic and Chisholm's Paradox (MATTHEW A. FERKANY); Contextual Influences on Wittgenstein's Philosophy (JONATHAN C. MESSINGER); Intuitions in Conceptual Shape? Misconceptions and Motivations (NATHAN C. DOTY); An Attack On Tradition (ROBERT ERLEWINE); Nietzschean Christology (CHRISTOPHER RODKEY); Heidegger, Lao Tzu and Dasein (CHRISTOPHER MARTIN); The Fractal Self and the Organization of Nature: The Daoist Sage and Chaos Theory (DAVID JONES AND JOHN CULLINEY); Reading Socially Engaged Buddhism in Modern America: A Case Study of Tibet/Tibetan Buddhism (JENNIFER MANLOWE).

2000 – 286 + xxii pages – ISBN 1-586840-42-8

Instant Nirvana

₨ **Strange Birds from Zoroaster's Nest:**
An Overview of Revealed Religions
Laina Farhat-Holzman

The Mystery of Human Religion; The Common Stream of Human Religion; Beyond Priests and Human Sacrifice: Human Responsibility; Good and Evil: No Shades of Gray; Unforeseen Consequences: The Transformed Message; State Religion: The Kiss of Death; The Role of Zoroastrian Heresies in Shaping Later Monotheistic Religions; Zoroastrian Concepts in World Religions; Zoroaster's Mark on the Secular World; The Modern Dilemma: A World Religion?; Epilogue: The Future of Religion; Appendix: Zoroastrian Texts and Scholarly Disagreements.

2000 – 236 + xiv pages – ISBN 1-586840-31-2

₨ **Philosophy and the Public Realm**
Douglas W. Shrader, editor

The Exhilarating Freedom! Hope in Existentialism (CHRISTINE M. CINQUINO); The Problem of Happiness in Nietzsche's "Use and Abuse of History" (MALINDA FOSTER); Tradition and Modern Meaning: Society and Relative Truth (JASON BAUMGARTH); Ethical Theory Reconsidered: An Evaluation of the Ethics of Health Care (RACHEL HOUCHINS); Proof of Paternal Rights in Abortion (MICHAEL ALAN PAYNE); Political Noise and Vociferous Silence: Heidegger and Nazism (TAMARA JOHNSON); Incommensurability, Normative Vices, and the Comparative Language Game: A Wittgensteinian Model for Comparative Philosophy (ERIN CLINE); Wittgenstein and Naturalism (ZACHARY HAINES); The Mask Unmasked: The Role of Hypocrisy in the Dialectic of *Thus Spoke Zarathustra* (JOHN KAAG); The Experience and Expression of Truth (JUSTIN C. MAAIA); On the Event of Truth: A Discussion of Art, Truth and the Primal Conflict in Heidegger's "The Origin of the Work of Art" (IAIN TUCKER BROWN); Towards a Processean Aesthetics Within a Whiteheadian Metaphysics (SCOTT M. GLEASON); Pragmatism and the Future of Confucianism in China (JOANNA CROSBY); Whose Democracy? Which Rights?

Ashok Kumar Malhotra

A Confucian Critique of Modern Western Liberalism (HENRY ROSEMONT, JR.).
2001 – 302 + xxvi pages – ISBN 1-586841-16-5

∞ **The Way of Poetry:**
Essays on Poetics and Contemplative Transformation
Patrick Laude

Introduction; Hindu Poetics: The Liberating Word; Islam: Sufism and Poetry; Lu Chi's *Wen Fu*: Poetry As Contemplation in the Chinese Classical Tradition; Japanese Poetry: The Sketch of Metaphysical Perception; Western Poetics: Inspiration, Self-Knowledge, and Spiritual Presence; Conclusion.
2002 – 244 + x pages – ISBN 1-58684-177-7

∞ **Thinking Outside the Box**
Douglas W. Shrader, editor

No-things that are Some-things: Democritus and Daoists on the Void (ERIN CLINE); The Hindu Problem of Evil, Suffering and Sin (DAVID TULKIN); The Highest Good – Happiness in Proportion to Virtue: A Kantian and Buddhist Ideal, or Reality? (JUSTIN C. MAAIA); A Representative Education (CAROLINE MARIE WATRAL); The Case for Post-Normal Science as an Integral Philosophy of Science (NATE ZUCKERMAN); Communication in a Practical Light (JOANNA DOODY); Wittgenstein's Rejection of the Private Language Argument: Implications for the Language-Game of Pain in the Therapeutic Relationship (ADRIAN M. VIENS); Reviving Fighting Words Doctrine: An Expansion of Hostile Environments (CHRISTOPHER LA-BARBERA); Beyond the Death of God: The Question of Nihilism in Nietzsche and Pascal (TUSHAR IRANI); Desire-(of)-Consciousness (JOHN BOVA); The Magico-Medicinal *Ethos* of Wine and Song in the Homeric *Hymn to Dionysos* (LINDA ARDITO); Observing Ritual "Propriety (*Li*)" as Focusing the "Familiar" in the Affairs of the Day (ROGER AMES).
2002 – 284 + xxvi pages – ISBN 1-58684-220-x

Instant Nirvana

ɞ Philosophical Dreams
Douglas W. Shrader, editor

Faith and Reason in Action: Abraham, Kierkegaard, and Incommensurability (MANCY PENDERGRASS); The Suffering of Innocents: A Reply to Ivan Karamazov (JOHN A. HOUSTON); Animal Rights in a Kantian Framework (JASON R. OHLIGER); Legitimacy in the Liberal State: Political, not Metaphysical (ADRIAN M. VIENS); Tractatus Musicus (KRISTIN BENTON-GUERRIERO); Originality and Art (J. JORDYNE WU); A Response to the Case Against Compositionality: Universal Sufficient Applicability Conditions (SARA L. FRIEDEMANN); Zeno, Motion and the Mathematics of Infinity (JUSTIN K. DIMMEL); Hume: A Most Successful Enquiry (JESSICA GORDON); Nietzsche and Socrates: 1869-1879 (ADAM AROLA); Nishida's Essential Tension: The Paradox of Experience (NATE ZUCKERMAN); Nagarjuna and Derrida: East and West Meet With Deconstruction? (LITSA E. WILLIAMS); Human Identity: Buddhist and Psychoanalytic Perspectives (JOHN M. KOLLER); Against the Natural-Artificial Distinction (JOSEPH C. PITT).

2003 – 304 + xl pages – ISBN 1-59267-026-1

ɞ Self and Society
Douglas W. Shrader, editor

The Trials of Job: A Personal Reflection on an Existential Problem (JOHN A. HOUSTON); The Possibility of St. Anselm (MARK BERNIER); Haiku: Here's Looking at You (BRETT BODEMER); Moism and Western Philosophy: Altruism vs. Egoism (EMILY MCRAE); The Inevitability of Skepticism (MELISSA KOZAK); Normative Values in Contextualism (JASON HILLS); To Whom Did You Grant the Paradigm, Mr. Kuhn? (JONATHAN DAVID PRICE); From Suspicion to the Repressive Hypothesis: The Structure of Power and Object in Foucault's *Madness and Civilization* and *The History of Sexuality: Volume I* (ANDREW HAO); Please Call it Euthanasia (SANDRA FINN); Kierkegaard: A Fairytale of Himself (LAURA STEWART); Mass Media, Attention Export, and the Colonization of Conscious-

Ashok Kumar Malhotra

ness: A Buddhist Perspective (PETER HERSHOCK); Revising Nature: Thoreau's Work in the Maine Woods (JUDY SCHAAF). 2004 – 294 + xl pages – ISBN 1-529267-076-8

Ᏸ Once More with Feeling
Douglas W. Shrader, editor

Transcending the Individual (LAURA GILLESPIE); Animal Liberation: A Critique of Singer's Argument (SEAN CUMMINGS); Jackson and Nagel on Consciousness (HEATHER MILLS); A Defense of Nozick's "Experience Machine" (NATHAN BALLANTYNE); Time, Divine Eternity, and the Problem of Creation (ANDREW MOON); Remarkable and Unremarkable Worlds (MARCELLO ANTOSH); Similarities Between Confucius and Aristotle (TAMAR CHRISTMAS); Zhuangzi, Kierkegaard and Evolutionary Psychology (TED FOX); Towards a Hermeneutics of Gender (MATTHEW LANDIS); Emotions: Expression, Responsibility and Self-Control (JOSEPHE MICHAEL VINCENT); Music and Political Identity (KATHLEEN M. HIGGINS); The Politics of Emotion (ROBERT C. SOLOMON).

2005– ISBN pending

Ᏸ A New Page: Moral Dilemmas,
Philosophical Reflections and Comparative Analysis
Douglas W. Shrader, editor

On Moral Permissibility of Cloning (NICK KASATKIN); Exposing The Military's Professional Dilemma (MARIE MONTESANO); The Resurgence of Mind: Active Epiphenomenalism and the Will (JOHN CONRAD ROBINSON); Cognition and the Environment (CRAIG ROXBOROUGH); Tautologies of Time: An Ayer-type Critique of Shoemaker's Temporal Vacuums (HEATHER MILLS); Substance, Actuality, and Motion in Aristotle's Metaphysics (EMANN ALLEBBAN); Nietzsche's Conception of Seriousness (KARL J. SOUTHGATE); Heidegger/Asian Thought (TRAVIS WADE HOLLOWAY); The *Logos* of the *Dao*: Exploring the Shared Philosophy of Heraclitus and Xunzi (ANTTI KASKO); It's Just Music (ZACHARY C.

Instant Nirvana

CALLAGHAN); Ibn Rushd or Averroës? How Not To Study Islamic Philosophy (TAMARA ALBERTINI); The Implications of the Origins of the *Daodejing* for Philosophy (RONNIE L. LITTLEJOHN).

2006– ISBN pending

ಏ Wisdom of the Tao Te Ching
Ashok Kumar Malhotra

This book offers a unique transcreation of Lao Tzu's classic text: *Tao Te Ching* in a language and style creatively used to appeal to beginning students as well as the general public. Eighty-one chapters, divided into two books, include GOING WITH THE FLOW, THE GREAT MOTHER, COMPASSION FOR OTHERS, THE FORCE WITHIN (TE), and LIFE AND DEATH. Forward by Douglas W. Shrader. Introduction by Ronnie L. Littlejohn.

2006 – 118 + xxix pages – ISBN 1-59267-059-8

ಏ Humanity: East and West
Douglas W. Shrader, editor

The Incompatibility of Parfitian Survival and Parfitian Morality (ASHLEY INGLEHART); Systematic Function and Heuristic: A Synthetic Methodology (JOSHUA EARLENBAUGH); Is Determinism Really as Deterministic as We Have Determined It to Be? (SHANNA HOLLICH); Autochthony: Heidegger, Meta-Philosophy and Meditation (JOSHUA WOLAK); "A Good Conversation": Plato's Symposium, Nietzsche and a Philosophical Eros (TOM MANGIONE); Strait Jackets, Blinders, and What are we really arguing about anyway? (STEFAN SHIRLEY); Dōgen's Genjō Kōan: Full of Deficiency, Deficient of Fullness (PHILLIP WALSH); Traditional Chinese Symbols of Reproduction as Reflected in Excerpts of Lao Tzu's Writings (QI LU); Lao Tzu, Heraclitus and a Transcendent Ethic (AARON CRELLER); "The Universe is a finger, all things are a horse": A Daoist Critique of Aristotle's Principle of Non-Contradiction (PAUL D'AMBROSIO); The Inhuman (PAUL SANTILLI); Comparative Philosophy: Theory and Praxis (HOPE K. FITZ).

2007– ISBN pending

Ashok Kumar Malhotra

๕ The Practice of Philosophy
Douglas W. Shrader, editor

Richard Rorty and the Theological Virtues (ASHLEEN MENCHACA KELLY); Why Lie? Why Not? A Frank Look at the Moral Status of Lying (MICHAEL D. ONDRICK); Toward a Virtue of Irresolution: An Exploration of Descartes' Practical Philosophy (NICHOLAS KOZIOLEK); Dualism in Dance (ALEJANDRA IANNONE); Montaigne, Plato, Philosophy, and Death (STEPHEN STROTHER); Endless Realization and Beginningless Practice: Zen Master Dôgen's Unity of Practice and Enlightenment (JAMES GIANGREGORIO); The Sage and the Superman (MATTHEW H. MUCCI); Satyagraha: Tracking a Cultural Exchange (SCOTT ZUKE); On Physics and Philosophy (MORGAN HARDY); Michel Foucault, Subject-Knowledge and the History of Systems of Thought (MEGAN JEAN REA); Abu Ghraib: A Foucaultdian Analysis (ROCCO CARBONE); Mental Processes and Meanings (CORIN T. FOX); Coping with the Disease of Philosophy (ANDREW WHITEHEAD); Understanding Philosophy of Technology through the Technology of Chess (JOHN HARTMANN).

2008– ISBN pending

Instant Nirvana

Journal

⁗ East-West Connections: Review of Asian Studies
David Jones, editor
Volume 1, Number 1: 2001 – ISSN 1592679994

Research Papers

⁗ The Logic Beneath the Caution: An Analysis of the Buddha's Responses to Questions About the Self
Douglas W. Shrader

1992 – 22 pages – ISBN 0-9633277-3-9

⁗ On Hindu Philosophies of Experience: Cults, Mysticism, and Meditations
Ashok K. Malhotra

1993 – 75 pages – ISBN 1-883058-03-1

⁗ Near-Death Experiences: Scientific, Philosophical, and Religious Perspectives
Douglas W. Shrader

1995 – 56 pages – ISBN 0-9633277-9-8

Department of Philosophy
SUNY-ONEONTA
Oneonta, NY 13820-4015
www.oneonta.edu/academics/philos/ops.html